But For the Shadows, Mexico is Color

Georgina Young-Ellis and Jonathan Ellis

Published by LTB Productions & Publishing, 2025.

While every precaution has been taken in the preparation of this book, the publisher assumes no responsibility for errors or omissions, or for damages resulting from the use of the information contained herein.

BUT FOR THE SHADOWS, MEXICO IS COLOR

First edition. March 15, 2025.

Copyright © 2025 Georgina Young-Ellis and Jonathan Ellis.

ISBN: 978-0983390985

Written by Georgina Young-Ellis and Jonathan Ellis.

To the people of Mexico

Prologue

It's two days before Christmas. My family has just arrived in town and raw sewage is gushing out of the downstairs toilet. I text the landlord but he is wholly uninterested. He claims to have made some small attempt to get ahold of a plumber, but that person cannot be reached. I text my neighbor. She has a reliable guy and we get him on the line. He says he'll be there soon. When is soon? I've got four people who have just made the trek from San Diego to Tijuana, from there by plane to Mexico City, and from there, via hired car, to San Agustín, our tiny town in Hidalgo, Mexico. It's ten in the morning; they've been traveling for six hours; they're tired, and of course, they all need the bathroom the moment they arrive. Some, including the landlord, might argue that this extra bathroom activity all at once was the cause for the overflow. The plumber, when he finally arrives, assures me it isn't.

I send three of them, my sister, her husband, and his sister off to their quaint hotel, and my mom stays put, somehow taking it all in stride. Jon and I are running around using every towel in the house to mop up the ever-expanding, and truly disgusting, flood. We use them up quickly as we only have four to our name. Jon runs out to the housewares store to buy a slew of these little throw rugs they tend to use in Mexico, which are somewhere between cleaning rags and doormats. He comes home with about ten of them and we finally have the flood under control, but it's seeped out into the living room and, man, it stinks.

It takes the plumber about two hours to get here and, once he arrives, determines the problem is not the toilet; it's much bigger. Of course it is. In the meantime, we can only use the upstairs toilet, but we cannot flush—or run any other water for that matter.

With a sledge hammer, the plumber starts opening the cement covers over the sewer line that runs under the patio we share with the neighbor, exposing more, and completely nauseating, raw sewage—the sewage that's been backing up there for who knows how long. It takes him about seven hours to fix it, which is pretty impressive to be honest. In the meantime, I tell my family to meet us for dinner at the only truly nice restaurant in town. I'm not about to cook with this horror going on.

By the time we get back from dinner he's got it fixed and we can use the bathrooms now, but not until we bag up all the towels and put them outside, and I scour every inch of the downstairs floor with white vinegar. We pay him 2,300 pesos, about $115 dollars, which, of course, for us, is nothing for that amount of work. Imagine what a plumber would cost to do this in the U.S. Still, by Mexican standards, it's a lot.

I let the landlord know it's fixed and what we paid, but he doesn't respond. By now I'm sure he's completely wrapped up in Christmas activities and, besides, the longer we've been in the house, the more of a penny pincher he's become. I'm pretty sure we won't see that money again, even though this repair was entirely his responsibility.

¡*Feliz Navidad!*

If you're wondering what brought us to this moment in time and this house in Mexico, well, the story begins before any of the 2,730,000 steps, which were taken during the nine months of one of the greatest adventures of our lives.

You see, I was awarded a Fulbright grant in 2022, to teach in Mexico for those nine months. I had earned my master's in Spanish Language and Literature a couple of years before at a much older age than most people do. Call me a late bloomer.

I decided to apply for the Fulbright about two years after I got my master's as we were emerging from the pandemic. I needed a jolt, something new, something exciting, and, frankly, something of a big accomplishment. But mostly, I wanted to conduct research in Mexico on emerging female Mexican writers. This was the focus of my application though my main work would be teaching English.

I applied in September of 2021, had an interview with the committee at my university in Portland, Oregon in November, was accepted by the Fulbright International Committee in January, and had an online interview with COMEXUS, the Mexican commission that handles the Fulbright grantees in Mexico, toward the end of February. March 21st, after a nail-biting month of waiting, I got the news. I had won the award. Prestigious as it is, please don't think I was the only one. There are around 56 English Teaching Assistant (ETA) Fulbright-Garcia Robles awards given each year for Mexico, most of them to much younger people than myself. I was the anomaly, partly because of my age, and partly because I would be bringing a "dependent," as they put it—in this case, my husband. Most ETAs are just out of college or graduate school and, as I later found out, none bring partners, although I wasn't the only one to bring a cat. I had no idea where I would be placed, other than somewhere in Mexico.

By July 1st, I had gotten all the details arranged to rent our house in Portland, but still didn't know where in Mexico I would be sent. Then, on July 6th, the email arrived in my inbox. I had my placement: San Agustín, Hidalgo, Mexico. My kid and their partner were visiting us at the time, and so I ran to find them and Jon, and tell them the news. We immediately starting Googling it. My excitement waned as I started looking at images of the town, and the university where I would be teaching: Universidad Politécnica Francisco I. Madero (UPFIM). The university looked small and old, but pretty. The town just looked small. In fact, it was—only 11,000 people in the municipality itself. We went onto Google Earth and started virtually wandering down streets and through the town square. My enthusiasm piqued again. It was cute—no tourist mecca, that's for sure, but that's what I'd wanted—a place to experience the real Mexico. This, I realized, was it. It was also clean looking and rather colorful. The town square was maybe a little sparse, but the nearby church was beautiful in that white, colonial way that Mexican churches sometimes are. I began to grow fond of the town, and kind of protective of it. Yeah, it was in a semi-arid region, yeah, it was above 6,000 feet, which meant the weather was probably a bit extreme; yeah, it was small, and fairly basic, but it was mine. It was going to be my home for nine months and I was sure I would love it.

One problem was that it was impossible to find housing online, other than a few Air B and Bs in towns about a half an hour away. They were all too expensive for permanent options and, besides, I wanted to be in, not near, San Agustín. Anyway, my contacts from the school were telling me I had to wait until we got there to connect with landlords face to face. People don't do business online, they said.

In the meanwhile, we had to get ourselves to the Visa office at the Mexican Consulate here in Portland. We hadn't been able to take care of that task until we knew our specific destination in Mexico. We felt confident when we reported to the woman across the desk that we were heading to San Agustín, Hidalgo. She had been taking notes as we spoke, and now she looked up and tapped the pen to her lips. "Never heard of it," she said. This was not the last time we were to hear these words over the next nine months. Still, she smiled and asked for a few moments in the outer office to see what she could do. In the time she was gone we shared a giddy laugh over the fact that one of the main requirements of receiving visas was to tell them exactly where we were going. No one in the office had ever heard of our town, but visas were issued anyway. We left in high spirits.

As July came to a close, and our departure date, August 28th, grew closer and closer, I began to panic. The school had promised me one week in a small house on campus, and I went ahead and rented an Air B and B for three weeks in one of those nearby towns, so that at least bought us a month. I still felt untethered. I wanted to get our housing situation nailed down. Apparently, that wasn't going to happen, and neither the Fulbright organization, nor COMEXUS, were responsible for helping with it.

Okay, that was just how it was going to be. We would find the place once we got there, keeping our fingers crossed. This is not how I like to do things. I'm a planner. I don't like to have my living details up in the air, especially in a foreign country.

And then there was the cat.

Let's not forget the cat.

We had decided several months before that we would bring Lupita, a very large grey kitty, about five years old, who isn't the most affectionate of creatures but who loves us nevertheless. Jon felt that to leave her with someone else would feel like abandonment to her, and she had been abandoned more than once, earlier in her life so we just couldn't do it. Nope, all fourteen pounds of her was coming with us.

After a summer of packing up all items in our house that we didn't want to leave for tenants to paw through, which included Jon building a shed in the garage that we named The Fortress of Solitude, where we would store it all, we got our visas together, packed winter and summer clothes and lots of other things we wouldn't need and, on the 28th of August at 10:00 in morning, boarded the plane, cat in tow, bound for Mexico City.

It was a tiring day of travel: fourteen hours, which included layovers and a long haul in customs, but Lupita was more chill than either Jon or I about it. When we got to the hotel room in Mexico City, she bounded out of the kitty-carrier, stretched out on the floor, and essentially said with her body language: "Ah, Meh-hee-coh!"

The next few days of Fulbright/COMEXUS orientation were rather a blur. I was jet-lagged, as I'm sure all other 55 ETAs in my cohort were, but we had to be up bright and early and in meetings by 8:00 am. The meetings were all day for two days, with about an hour and a half in the middle for lunch, that is, if everything went on time, which it didn't. The whole thing made me cranky since I don't like meetings, nor not having at least some autonomy over my own time, but we had no choice. These orientations were part of our grant and we had to participate under threat of not getting all our scholarship money.

In the meantime, Jon was out roaming around Mexico City with very little knowledge of Spanish, finding a permanent litter box for Lupita, sand, and food for her beyond what we had brought with us, a blow dryer for me, and various snacks to keep me going.

On the evening of the second day, attendance at a welcoming party at a nearby modern art museum was mandatory for all ETAs. All the COMEXUS bigwigs were there, mingling and chatting with everyone, making sure we felt welcome. Snacks were endlessly passed around on silver platters by a staff of well-organized wait people, and copious amounts of wine flowed. No glass was allowed to reach the halfway point. Speeches were given with elaborate ceremony to tremendous applause. Mariachis in silver bespangled turquoise uniforms marched in with a fanfare of trumpets to provide some of my favorite entertainment. I love Mariachis but this, along with everything else, was way over the top. I have no idea what time the event eventually broke up because we saw an opportunity and quietly ducked out early.

On the third and final day of orientation, representatives from the school where each ETA would be teaching came to get us.

Everyone was placed in a location between 1-6 hours from Mexico City, though some were placed right in CDMX (Ciudad de México). Others had to get back on planes to get to their placements, but most of us were picked up in Mexico City by a person designated as our "tutor," from our host institution. This was a big moment, accompanied by a big ceremony, complete with photo ops, as we met our tutors. Mine was a sweet young woman named Lina. Shortly after meeting her, one of my first cultural faux pas occurred, the first of many that I made over the nine months I was in Mexico.

As Jon and I gathered our stuff together in the hotel lobby: four suitcases, the cat in her carrier, litter box, stacks of teaching materials from COMEXUS, and various other extra bags of things we'd already acquired, I noticed this fellow sort of hanging out near Lina. She introduced him to me as Alberto, with no other explanation.

"Is he the driver?" I asked her. "Driver" by the way, is *chofer* in Spanish.

"No," she replied drily, "he's a teacher at the school. He'll be helping me navigate."

I was mortified beyond belief, but it ultimately became a joke between me and Alberto, who had a great sense of humor, and who henceforth referred to himself as my chauffer.

Lina turned out to be an excellent driver. Jon, also a great driver himself, commented on this, making note that, although he had driven in many very busy and confusing places, he would never attempt driving in this city. It feels, he said, like the drivers here are working with some sort of telepathy in their collection of skills. Accidents constantly seemed imminent with such things as crazy left turns from right lanes, yet we never witnessed a single incident. The three-hour drive through the crowded city, beyond its outskirts, and to San Agustín was part excitement and part exhaustion. Lupita, as was now customary, took it all in stride.

Once we crossed the border into Hidalgo, the landscape became more scenic: high but green desert, lots of agriculture, along with vast, verdant spaces. After we cleared Pachuca, the state capital, it became downright spectacular with mountains sprouting large rock formations that jutted into the air. Alberto informed us they are called, Los Frailes, the Friars. An interesting name because they do rather resemble tall, dour monks. More about this later.

About a half an hour beyond Pachuca, we hit Actopan (pronounced Oct-TOH-pahn). In previous communications with Lina, she urged me to look for a rental in Actopan, which is where she lives. She felt the rent was cheaper, which I ultimately didn't find to be true, and that there were more options, which definitely was true. I was determined not to cave though. Jon and I both really wanted to live in San Agustín, partly due to its close proximity to the school, but, as I mentioned, we were already fond of it, sight unseen. Besides, I didn't like the look of Actopan—just another crowded city, in my mind. Later, I'd come to change that opinion.

We entered Actopan and soon turned off onto another highway leading to San Agustín. We passed many small, somewhat shabby-looking towns and lurched over endless speedbumps. There aren't many police on the highways but they keep things under control with speedbumps. There are a lot of them. The landscape was still very pretty, but the look of those towns along the highway had me praying San Agustín was going to be different.

We stopped at an OXXO, one of the ubiquitous convenience-stores that dot Mexico—kind of like a 7/11—to get a few supplies: oatmeal, milk, eggs, bacon, lunch meat, butter and whatnot. Bread, by the way, is not a staple to be found in any convenience store in small Mexican towns. At this point, we were still on the outskirts of San Agustín, so we really weren't able to get a feel for it. Then a few moments later, back on the road, we passed a faded sign painted on a dilapidated wall: I <3 S. Agus.

We were home.

Lina drove us through some narrow roads into the town and we were pleased with the place in the same way we had been when we saw it on Google Earth: it was cute. Then, she stopped at a restaurant, one that looked to be nice, and they said they would be treating us to dinner. It was about 5:00, my stomach hurt, and all I could really think about was getting Lupita out of the carrier. We thanked them profusely, but declined. We just wanted to get to the campus house.

In five more minutes, we were there. I had seen some pictures of the interior, so I knew it would be basic, and it was, but it was shelter. I let Lupita out of her bag and she sniffed around, unimpressed. In fact, it was a bit dusty and unkempt. Lina assured us that someone would be in the next day to clean, but at least the beds were made with clean linens and there were a couple of towels handy.

Jon took a peek into the bathroom and announced: "There's no toilet seat!"

"Oh, we don't use them here," Lina replied.

Jon and I glanced surreptitiously at one another, astonished. That was something we hadn't expected. Why would we?

Lina and Alberto bade us farewell, and we were left to make further discoveries on our own, most notably: dishes, silverware, cookware, glasses, utensils, or anything of any sort to cook or eat with were nowhere to be found. We quickly verified that the stove didn't work, though there was a microwave. We had food, but no way to prepare it, nor plates to eat it on. We were a good mile and a half from any restaurants (that we didn't know about anyway, nor how few there really were) and too exhausted to walk it, and, trust me, there's no Uber. Also, we had no wi-fi, internet, or phone connection to call someone.

At this point, our only option was to wander around the isolated and deserted campus to try to at least find some wi-fi. No luck.

We finally saw a lady walking by and approached her to see if she had a connection. She did. Lovely person that she was, she stopped what she was doing and called Rico, the English Department head and, essentially, my boss, to tell him the problem. He said he'd alert the campus housekeeping. About an hour later, the security guard arrived with a bag of dishes and cooking implements—nothing fancy, but they would do. Thankfully, we were set, for the moment anyway. We ended our first day in San Agustín with a meal cobbled together with what we had on hand, and figured we'd deal with the stove and whatever else the next day, very grateful for the kindness of strangers who saved us from going to bed hungry that night. Okay, yes, we could have gobbled pieces of lunch meat with our fingers like the savages we were fast becoming. And sure, let's face it, if push came to shove, we would have done that. We were very thankful, however, to everyone involved that we didn't have to, while acknowledging to one another we're nothing if not resilient.

We each took a shower, without any knowledge whatsoever of what a luxury it was. There would be no hot water in the morning

Lupita, for her part, wandered around the house for a while, and, then, to our surprise, became bored, and jumped back into the dreaded kitty carrier. She spent the rest of the evening playfully leaping in and out of it. What had once been her four-pawed, spread-eagle resistance to the thing, now became her solace against a place clearly not designed for kitties. She kept us entertained. We were all embracing Mexico.

40,000 to 60,000 Steps

The cleaning crew arrives in the morning to spruce things up. I ask about possibly arranging for someone to check on the hot water and gas for the stove, tentatively suggesting that these things might somehow be related? No one seems to know anything. They say to ask Doña Tina, the lady in charge of housekeeping for the entire school. She shows up to check on the progress of the cleaners and agrees to look into it. I remember to tell her we have no hot water. She says they have to alert security to turn it on each morning. Security, really? Okay, that would be terrific, I say. I also ask if there's a place to get laundry done. She doesn't know. So, before we head into town, we wander around in the tiny community that's just beyond the school gates, called Los Filtros (essentially, "the sewers," because a smelly canal runs through it), hauling a pillowcase full of laundry. We ask around and are told there's a lady who does take in laundry, you just have to knock on the big gate up the street. We do, and a sweet young woman takes our laundry, letting us know it will be about 120 pesos, and she'll have it done tomorrow.

Satisfied, Jon and I catch the combi into town, basically a van tricked out with bench seats around the sides of the interior, for which you pay ten pesos, depending on where you're coming from and where you're going. From the university into San Agustín, like I said, about a mile and a half, it's just the ten. We want to get a feel for the town and see if we can find some more food of some kind. You may be wondering: how hard is that to do in Mexico? Not hard, in general, but since there's nothing we can get on campus, as school hasn't started up yet and everything is closed, we want to make sure we have plenty of bottled water (an absolute must in Mexico) and stuff we can make in the microwave. We aren't confident the combi will run all weekend, and the walk from school into town is a long one. Also, we've been advised not to eat street food, and we aren't sure yet what constitutes street food since we quickly discover that San Agustín has very few restaurants, and prepared foods like tacos and tamales are sold from carts on the street or in what can only be described as a food court in one of the main buildings in the center of town.

One of our very first discoveries, near where the combi lets us off, is a tortillería where women are making corn tortillas by hand on a large griddle called a *comal*. Jon takes a video of them and they clearly think he's insane; at least, there's a lot of giggling going on. To them, what they're doing is the normal repetitive hot and sweaty work of the day. To us they are artisans creating works of wonder that speak to the soul. Perception is a funny thing. The tortillas are slapped on the hot surface, puff-up and then settle back as the women quickly tap them, flattening them back into their proper form. All of this is done with fingers. What's a spatula or a pair of tongs to these women? They are mistresses of the *comal*!

We definitely want to order but don't know in what quantity. We are certainly new in town. At this particular point they see us as visitors from space. We finally figure out by watching those ahead of us in line that half a kilo is about twenty tortillas—which cost eleven pesos. That's about sixty cents. They go in Jon's backpack. He complains they are so hot they are burning his back where it touches. What a baby. He repositions the pack to carry it on one shoulder. Problem solved. To be fair, there are no longer twenty tortillas in the package. Two are conspicuously missing. We inhale them as we continue our explorations.

At a little store, packaged refried beans, tuna, and mayo are added to the pack. In another shop, bulk-salt and a bottle of hot-sauce join the rest of the collection. We now have the fixin's for at least a lunch and a dinner.

Necessities in check, we have time to wander around the town some more, exploring the church, just getting the lay of the land. Everywhere we go, we attract attention. Jon is rather dark complected so he figured he'd fit in more than me. But it's the little things: the fact that he wears sweat pants, t-shirts, sneakers and either a sun hat or a baseball cap, and sunglasses. The men here simply don't dress like that. They wear slacks or jeans, mostly button down or polo type shirts, and boots. Almost no one wears sunglasses or hats unless they're cowboy hats, or big, straw sun hats. He does not fit in. But me, oh my god, I attract the kind of attention a giraffe would if one suddenly appeared in the midst of this little Mexican town. Tall, red-headed, blue-eyed, and freckled, they've literally never seen anything like me. It doesn't help that I've picked up a green umbrella for the sun because it calls even more attention to me. The point is, San Agustín is not a tourist town. No one from outside of Mexico visits here. Most of the time, there aren't even Mexican tourists here. This is a somewhat out-of-the-way farming community. The people you see here are the people who live here. Though some here might have seen someone as pale as I am on TV or in the movies, or maybe, if they've traveled or even visited Mexico City, they've seen Americans or Europeans, most have not. It's hard to get used to the stares, at times open-mouthed astonishment, as I walk by. Children in particular, whose mothers don't bother to reign them in because they're also gawking, stare from every sidewalk and corner. Jon and I soon learn to disarm them with a smile and a "*buenos días*," or "*buenas tardes*." This does the trick because Mexican people tend to be very polite. We discover, to our delight, that even the toughest looking tough guys leaning on the wall smoking a cig, perhaps staring hard at the Americanos in distrust, which they have every right to feel, will check themselves, straighten-up, hide their smokes, and respond with an equally friendly response. I would say that people here have been trained (by Mama) to be polite. If someone greets you, you greet them back, even when they do look like they just fell off the mother-ship.

Speaking of mothers, when we get back to the university, I'm determined to call mine, whom I haven't spoken to since before we left the States. I'm sure she's dying to know what has become of us though I have sent her texts and photos, and she and others have been keeping up with us on Facebook and Insta. Yet, here I am, faced with the same dilemma as the day before. There is no available communication of any kind.

How do I get enough service to call her? We have brought with us a portable hotspot, but it still needs a signal to get wi-fi, and I can only call if I have wi-fi. We have special sim cards to use in Mexico, though I don't understand all that stuff well enough to explain it to you, so at least we can use our phones, but we still need a connection to make a call.

From Jon: Although I'm participating as a filler-in-of-details and things forgotten with Geo on this project, sometimes I will speak directly on various subjects. This is the first of these interjections: I did purchase a "portable hotspot." It's a device about the size and weight of my phone that takes its own local sim-card (BTW here a sim-card is called a "chip") to be differentiated from the "special" international sims provided for our phones by our U.S. phone provider. We must have them, they've informed us, to have service while in Mexico. Clearly enough, for all the scavenger-hunt type chasing around required to get them, they do not work. Let's just say they lied, and were very happy to spend my time and gas while doing so. The chip in the hotspot, on the other hand, is from a local phone provider that, in theory, provides local service to the area. The problem we're encountering is that, in this particular place on the UPFIM campus, there is no phone service of any kind. This makes the portable hotspot a portable dead-weight that needs to be carried around for no reason whatsoever. It also makes me want to call our (explicative removed) U.S. phone provider to scream at them. Naturally, there is no way to call them. Catch-22 in real time. Aaaarugh!

One of the things I want to mention about the canal Geo mentioned and how bad it smells is not to point out that this is a problem specific to Mexico. I can attest to having walked through Times Square on a nice summer evening to the reek of sewage wafting from the local sewer grate.

I go out wandering around with my umbrella, in the heat, trying to find a building to snuggle up to where I can get a connection. I finally do, next to the main building of the school where, of course, there is no shade. Also, and this is something that really puzzles me about the school, there's no outdoor public seating anywhere, except for some cement tables and stools in front of what they call a cafeteria. I don't know what kind of food they'll have in said cafeteria since, along with everything else, it's not open. Anyway, there's no grassy "quad" where students might comfortably sit to read or do homework while watching their classmates enjoy a friendly game of frisbee or hacky-sack. There are no shaded benches placed outside the buildings, or anywhere else, where friends or couples could perhaps meet and schmooze, not even a lawn for quick picnics. Other than that, it's quite a pretty campus where sunflowers, corn, and lavender grow in abundance. The lack of lawn bothers me in spite of my understanding that lawns in general are not very eco-friendly. However, on a big campus like this a lawn would serve to at least provide a place to park. Yes, it's all about me.

At any rate, the two main buildings are mostly modern though not fancy, while the library is actually quite impressively modern. The building that shows up when you Google the university, the one that had me thinking the school was small and old, is actually not used anymore by UPFIM.

I sit on the hard cement with my back against the wall and call Mom. How wonderful it is to hear her voice and tell her all the details of our first few days in Mexico. She is so excited about this adventure of ours and wants to know everything. In fact, she and my sister have already decided to come visit us for Christmas though we have no house yet, and don't know what those arrangements will be like. This gives me incentive. We'll have to find a place with two or more bedrooms and, ideally, more than one bathroom. We will want visitors. We already love San Agustín and want to share it with everyone.

From Jon: I have a wonderful photo of Geo sitting against the wall under her green umbrella. I am perhaps a hundred yards away. In film, a shot like this, showing an individual alone against a vast background translates to a sense of isolation. It works perfectly in this photo. Geo is beautiful, and beautifully lit, in stark contrast to the white wall.

And so, the day winds down and we eat tacos for dinner: fresh tortillas, bacon we cooked in the microwave, refried beans, and avocado. They are divine.

60,000 to 80,000 Steps

Sunday, we make another foray into San Agustín to find an ATM, this time, walking the mile and a half because we're very low on cash and cannot afford the combi. We only have enough to pay for our laundry, which we'll pick up on the way home.

There's a fair going on in town, complete with booths, rides, and junk food. On top of that, it's market day, a brand-new phenomenon for us. Though the fair monopolizes the center of town, the market squeezes in around the edges: stands upon stands of vendors selling fruits, vegetables, meats, housewares, clothing, shoes, leather goods, spices, herbs, cooked prepared foods with tables and chairs where you can sit and eat, toys, stationary, flour tortillas—a rarity it seems—artisanal cheeses, eggs, milk, local produce such as *nopales*—prickly pear paddles cleaned of their spines—squash blossoms, the flower of the agave plant called *gualumbos*, and buckets of squirming little red worms called *chinicuiles*. The venders assure us they're delicious. I'm sorry (or not sorry) to say I won't be trying them. There are tablecloths, aprons, dishrags, cleaning supplies, grocery items, flowers, CDs, electronics, used tools, underwear, sportswear, and all kinds of random geegaws and widgets. On the side streets of the town there are second-hand items for sale, set up on blankets along the roads or under awnings, especially clothes and tools, but also baskets, furniture, and more food.

We are pleasantly overwhelmed by all this activity. The colors, both of the wares and the tarps overhead are brilliant. The hawkers call to us: "Mango, *piña* (pineapple), *sandía* (watermelon), papaya…. *Güera! Güerita! Bonita!* they call to me, meaning, "White girl, little white girl, pretty girl!" I giggle. I'm hardly a girl, but it gets my attention. I smile at them, flattered, on some level. On another level, I'm fully aware of the "colorism" behind these greetings. I've known for many years that anyone with lighter skin or hair than average gets called *güera*, or *güero*—the male version (pronounced WHERE-ah/oh), as if being whiter makes them more special. The darker skinned people don't get a special name unless they're really dark, then they are called *morenito/a*. This distinction based on color makes me sad. And yet, every time anyone calls me *güerita*, my head turns and I smile. I can't help it; it sounds so loving; it's such an endearment. Still, I know better. I have to do better.

No matter how enticingly they call out to us, we can't buy anything because we have zero money. We are heading to one of the four ATMS in town to get some cash so we can get more groceries, which we would love to purchase here in the market. First, we head to the bank, the only one in town. We try the ATM. Empty. No cash. Trying not to panic, we go across the plaza to one of the other ATMS. No cash. We walk to the other side of the block where there are two ATMS right next to each other. People walk away from the machines shaking their heads. "*No hay efectivo.*" "There's no cash." Now what?

There are a few small grocery stores in town, chain stores called 3B. They are a little more well stocked than the OXXO, but not by much. The OXXO, by the way, is too far to walk. We head into one of the 3Bs to find they do not accept credit cards. Almost no one does in this town. What we really need is a store where we can get groceries as well as cash back.

We come upon a friendly policeman who informs us that every Sunday is market day, using the word *tianguis*, which is new to me. He tells us that the ATMs run out of cash because the town fills up on *tianguis* day, this particular Sunday made worse because of the fair. He says that, to get cash back with a credit card, we have to go to a big grocery store called Aurera. It's a couple of blocks, just up this road, he tells us. Relieved, we start walking, practicing saying *tianguis* (prounounced tee-AHN-gheese though Jon memorizes it by saying "tea and geese"). We walk, and walk, and walk: six blocks, eight, ten, twelve. We begin to wonder if maybe it was closed and we missed it. We are really on the outskirts now and wondering if the store even exists. Finally, exhausted and hungry, we come upon the place. Jon is carrying a backpack and is told he can't go in. So I go in and rustle up everything I can find that isn't too heavy to carry though I'm inspired at the thought that, with the cash back, we'll be able to catch one combi into the town center, and the one from there to the university. In fact, with cash, we can get all kinds of things at the *tianguis*, and maybe even venture to try some of the street food.

I get up to the cashier with bread, lettuce, more tuna, ham, almond milk (yay!), a bottle of water, potato chips to scarf down now because I'm starving, and a few other various and sundry things. I'm happy and relieved to find that the card works. And yet, no cash back. Not with this type of card, this AMERICAN card. I'm despondent as I go to tell Jon. Now, we have to walk all the way back into town and all the way to the university. As I go to fish a tissue out of my pocket, I discover 40 pesos there, above and beyond the laundry money. Glory hallelujah! It's just enough for each of us to take the two combis that will get us home and not have to use the laundry money. We cram potato chips into our mouths and chug the water as we wait for the combi, huddling under the green umbrella because the sun is searing.

We make it home and collapse for a while before going to get our laundry, which is fresh and more beautifully folded than any laundry I've ever seen.

From Jon: when Geo went into the store, I found a rectangle of shade on the cement in front. I sat and people-watched. They watched back. Some smiled, others pretended not to see me after they obviously had. Curious children asked their mothers what they were seeing. For my part I watched a guy in a long-sleeved, gray security uniform (that had to be blazing hot), whose purpose seemed to be unnecessarily directing traffic in and out of the lot. It really wasn't very busy. Perhaps this was a quiet time of day? In this asphalt-covered entertainment-vacuum, he occupied himself, dancing along to music playing loudly from a little radio in his pocket. He incorporated his arm-swinging into directing cars. Frankly, this guy was a pretty cool customer under the blazing sun. It reminded me of NYC traffic cops directing traffic in a similar way, but in huge bustling intersections. I thought to video him, but found it impossible. Each time I had the camera ready to go, he would stop. I think maybe he knew.

80,000 to 130,000 Steps

The fall semester at school has started. This morning, I'm required to attend an outdoor opening ceremony that starts at 9:00 am. As all the teachers and the entire student body gather in the blazing sun, already hot at this hour, the national and state anthems are sung, the color guard presents the flag accompanied by a squawky bugle corps, speeches are given, and awards handed out. I've got my umbrella so I'm good, but after about an hour of this, I see the students begin to wilt.

After that, I attend a teachers' meeting, where we rate potential English books to use as soon as they can be ordered. This is the kind of thing I'm very familiar with and I'm happy to be included in the decision-making process.

As I'm busy with these activities, which last until about noon, Jon is out and about in Los Filtros looking for rental options. It's not that we want to live in Los Filtros, but it's super close to the school, and if we find someplace nice, why not grab it? Lina told me she saw a sign in that area advertising apartments for rent, so Jon has gone in search of it. During those three hours or so, he's managed to make friends with a guy who works for the telephone company. He has a small, company-provided truck and, in the middle of his work day, invited Jon to get in the truck to go see a place that he knew about. Sadly, the lead didn't pan out. Turned out the brothers who owned the house were having an argument and couldn't figure out what they wanted to do.

From Jon: I met Topiltzin as I wandered about Los Filtros looking for a For Rent sign that was supposed to be in the area. He was working on a large box of wiring. I was feeling pretty comfortable with making myself understood and understanding, but the first thing I asked him was, "Do you speak English?" He said a little. It turned out he was wrong in his estimation of his level of proficiency. His English is very good. I asked, since he was a person who was driving around the area, if he knew about the sign I was looking for. He did not, but he said he might know of a place fairly nearby. "Wonderful. Can you tell me where?" What he said next absolutely blew me away. He told me to go ahead and get in his work truck and in a few minutes, he would take me to the house. He literally stopped in the midst of his work to help a random stranger. Would this ever have happened in any place I have ever lived? Possibly in Santa Fe, New Mexico 30 years ago, but nowhere else. My first friend in Mexico!

A bit more about this Los Filtros area: it smells like a sewer because, essentially, that's what it is. (And, yes, I was looking for a place to rent in this area, because it's near the school. Necessity can be very inspiring.) Anyway, this is essentially the source, other than rain, used to water crops. It's named quite literally what it is: a filter. The whole area is filtering the run-off from Mexico City. It contains not only sewage, but heavy metals, pharmaceuticals and all kinds of contaminates. Even upon arrival, one thing had already and quite thoroughly filtered into our thoughts: we could not drink water from the tap. Almost no one does, not even the locals. Everyone knows this to the degree that not a single person would even think to provide visitors with this vital piece of information, because, as I said, everyone knows. Water in Mexico comes in bottles. Every home has a stand for the big five-gallon jugs with a bomba *(pump) which rests on top of the bottle. Water in the U.S. is a utility. Water in Mexico is an industry. Someone, clearly in the "let's deliver water" industry, made this brilliant decision about 50 years ago and it stuck. It drives home how important water is. We all know the idea of water being life, and yet, a lot is done to it that makes it anti-life. The big bottles are not that expensive, five gallons for fourteen pesos (about seventy cents). Still, as I said, almost no one drinks water from the tap. The very poor have no choice. I am forced to imagine they die quite young.*

We finally get a lead on a house, a big house, by all accounts, literally around the corner from the school. The sign that had been previously mentioned was actually on that house, but had been blocked when someone closed a shutter, making it unreadable from the street. Anyway, after a few text messages back and forth, we get an appointment with a guy who meets us there. It doesn't take long to determine that this place was an abandoned funeral parlor, as the fading sign in front indicates. It's advertised as 4 bedrooms, 2 baths and goes for 7,000 pesos a month—an astonishing amount of money for rent in this area.

We enter through a filthy and dilapidated kitchen, and pass through to the living room, a large, round space, also filthy. We look up to see that a balcony, if you want to call it that, runs around the perimeter of the second floor, overlooking the living room. "Overlooking," is no exaggeration. It overlooks it with no impediment of anything like a railing, or banister, or anything else that would keep you from plunging to your death with one misstep. Apparently, that's where the bedrooms are located. The guy showing it to us enthusiastically points out a disgusting mattress leaning against the wall of the death-walk, which, according to him, designates the place as "furnished." I do my level-best to politely let him know we're not interested, and we high-tail it out of there.

We're feeling discouraged but, before we left Portland, I'd found an apartment for rent via Facebook in the nearby town of Progreso. It has the required three bedrooms and one and a half baths, and doesn't look too bad though it is completely unfurnished. Rico agrees to take us there the next day to see it.

Around three in the afternoon, after Rico frees up some time, we head to Progreso in his car, about 15 minutes away (or 45 minutes by bus). We soon arrive and find the address. It's down a dirt road, next to an abandoned-looking construction site. The owner meets us there and takes us in for a tour. It's green. Really green. Every surface inside and out is lime green. Lots of green walls. Okay, there is a touch of yellow here and there, and the floors are a tan marble. The rooms are small, the staircase to the second floor is claustrophobically narrow, and the bathrooms are miniscule. I'm trying to convince myself to like it because I'm worried we won't find anything else. As I discuss terms with the owner, Jon is staring at me, appalled. This is where he would be hanging out all day working (he teaches and does consultations on line). The view from upstairs, where his potential office would be, is of razor-wire, threatening atop every surrounding wall. At the construction site, a couple of weather-worn, flat-tired trucks accept their final resting place, and a few ne'er-do-wells hang out outside the liquor store diagonally across the street. The look on his face convinces me this will not do.

And so Rico drives us back into San Agustín and to the restaurant that Lina and Alberto wanted to take us to that first day. As soon as we walk in, we are filled with awe. In the midst of this unassuming little town is this oasis, a beautiful, lush green lawn, and, beyond, the dining room, flanked by floor to ceiling windows. Stunned, we take in the stone walls, high ceilings, and world class art on display throughout. The food is amazing and Rico's company delightful. He, by the way, speaks perfect English. He says not to give up—we'll find the right place, he's sure of it.

However, by the end of our first week, we still have not. And so, we gather up our ever-growing collection of suitcases and other possessions and, with Rico's help and that of another teacher, Manuel, we head to the Air B and B I rented in the town of Mixquiahuala (pronounced Meex-kia-WAlla), about ten minutes beyond Progreso by car (or an hour and twenty minutes by bus.)

We have a hard time finding the place. By the time we do, Rico has to get going, so he leaves us on the sidewalk of the very busy thoroughfare with our myriad suitcases and Lupita. We stand there waiting for the lady who had agreed to meet us to come let us in. Manuel refuses to leave us. If worse comes to worse, he says, we'll come stay with him and his family. We end up calling her and, eventually, a lady does come, a strong young woman who helps us haul our crap and the cat up to the second floor. At first glance, the place is nice looking. At second glance, once we've settled in a bit, we realize it's actually kind of shabby and it stinks. Like a sewer. In fact, the whole building does. So does the entire block. It must be sitting over some kind of exposed sewer main. Yet, it's all we have for now so we'd better get used to it. We could be here for another three weeks.

From Jon: The woman who came to let us in insisted on helping us with our bags. I told her they were heavy (each one literally weighed fifty pounds or, at this point, even more). I needn't have bothered. She picked up a bag in each hand and ran up the stairs like the athlete she clearly was. I was super impressed.

130,000 to 200,000 Steps

Mixquiahuala is a hell-hole. No, I'm sorry, that's not fair. The town is congested with that busy street that runs through it, and a center plaza that is underwhelming, nowhere near as cute as San Agustín's. But hell-hole is extreme. Along the main corridor are lots of shops where we manage to find some things we need, plus a few coffee places where Jon is able to get a half-way decent mocha in the morning. There is also a sweet little café at the junction of the avenue and the *centro* where we end up eating a couple of times because they have decent sandwiches and the owner is lovely.

We hate our Air B and B though, absolutely hate it. You know a place is bad when the cat hates it too. There are no accessible windows for her to look out of and I'm sure she's well aware of the stench. Also, having to take the bus or combi to and from San Agustín is a total drag. There's always a traffic jam somewhere between Progreso and Mixquiahuala, and the ride is hot and dusty.

As a result, we are all the more motivated to find a place in San Agustín. As the second week of school begins, I still don't have a teaching schedule but I've got lots of other things to take care of. Number one is finding a house or apartment, and number two is opening a bank account. This is an urgent matter because my first payment from COMEXUS is coming up at the end of September, and they've told us we won't get paid if we don't have a Mexican bank account.

From Jon: I got a line on some apartments for rent, as it turns out, in the same building as the funeral home, but owned by different people. They weren't apartments, exactly. I had to go up a spiral iron stairway, which was just a series of iron slats (there were no steps, just the slats which in theory, anyway, would support actual steps). This should have clued me in to what I was about to see. I arrive at the top of the stairs to find myself in a kind of hallway open to the street on one side. On the other side are two open doorways. They were open due to the fact that they had no doors. I now know "Se Renta Cuarto" posted on a random tree, means Room for Rent, but I didn't know that before this excursion into the Twilight Zone. I felt obligated to at least look into the rooms, since I'd bravely made it to the top of the so-called stairs. One was perhaps eight-by-ten and the other maybe ten feet square. The smaller room was furnished: it had a frayed, greying and very flat old mattress on the bare floorboards. The guy seemed puzzled, either by my having looked at all, or by the fact that I didn't seem to appreciate all that he was offering. I hightailed it out of there right behind the bedbugs who had moved out earlier due to unsanitary conditions.

I gird my loins and march into the one and only bank in San Agustín, which happens to be a Santander. I am told to sit in a row of chairs to wait for the person in charge of opening accounts. There's only one. She's a young woman dressed in a very tight suit with a short skirt, and high, high, platform heels. Every time she gets up to make a copy or whatever, she click-clacks across the floor, and I wonder how uncomfortable those shoes must be. Her co-worker is dressed exactly the same but, though she clacks around a lot, I don't know what her job is because she's not helping the people like me, waiting to open accounts. There's a teller at the window, but she's of no use to those of us waiting in the row of chairs. I wait for exactly two hours while the older couple just before me in line opens a bank account— their first ever, evidently—until it's finally my turn. The woman looks at my paperwork with very little interest and tells me I have to have my non-resident immigration card before I can open an account. I was afraid of that. Could COMEXUS have alerted me to this necessity when they insisted on the need for a Mexican bank account? Of course, they could have but they did not. To get our immigration cards, we must travel by bus to Pachuca, an hour and fifteen minutes away.

Fuming, I go to meet Jon at a little coffee place we've found in San Agustín, called Cafée Rinkon, which means Corner Café, spelled ironically wrong. I don't drink coffee, but Jon tells me theirs is at least acceptable, though not even close to his high standards. If you haven't guessed by now, my wonderful husband is a piece of work. There I find him, sitting at a booth *yukking* it up with a couple of *compadres* he's managed to connect with. One speaks English, the other doesn't, but they're all having a great time as if they've been friends forever. The one that doesn't speak English is the owner of the café, a big, burly guy named Marco. As I join the conversation in Spanish, I discover he also owns a house nearby, which he could conceivably rent, he tells me, in that it's been standing empty for three years. I immediately ask him when we can see it, and he tells me we can meet him there that very evening.

In the meantime, Rico has drummed up two possible apartment rentals, which we go with him to see early in the afternoon. Let me just say they'd do if nothing else comes up, and one of them may have to because we're pretty much done living in Mixquiahuala. The problem is these apartments, both in the same building, are on the second and third floors respectively, with very steep stairs, up which we'd have to haul our increasingly heavy suitcases and cat (she's digging the Mexican version of Friskies) and all the furniture we'd have to buy or rent because, of course, they're unfurnished. "Unfurnished" means also without refrigerator or stove. Beyond that, each of them only has one bathroom. I'm determined to have at least that extra half bath. We tell the guy we'll let him know the next day. I'm excited to see the house that Marco has and I'm praying it will be the answer.

Later that afternoon, we go with Rico to his parents' house where we've been invited for dinner. His parents are the sweetest people and his mom has prepared for us the specialty of this season throughout Mexico, *Chiles en nogada*. The dish is made with a Poblano chile, stuffed with ground meat, nuts, and a variety of spices. It's covered with cream, and topped with pomegranate seeds, thus displaying the Mexican colors, green, red, and white. Independence Day is September 15th, which is tomorrow, in fact, and all of Mexico comes alive with its national colors during this month.

I'm a little worried about eating the chile, afraid it will be very spicy. I haven't mentioned this yet, but I'd been struggling with a condition called interstitial cystitis, and I'm not supposed to eat anything spicy. To help deal with it, my doctor had me off any spicy foods, citrus, vinegars, alcohol, fermented foods, and anything that might cause a flare up. She's tried numerous treatments for me including therapies, various teas, potions, and medications, acupuncture, etc., and I really haven't seen an improvement. I was very annoyed that I'd be going to Mexico having to stay away from chiles, tomatoes, and lime, the cornerstones of much Mexican cuisine. So, I nibble at the chile, discovering it's a little spicy, but not too bad. I eat it, and then have another, partly because I want to be polite, and partly because it's delicious.

After dinner, we go to see Marco's house, just a block from Caféè Rinkon. The outside is unimpressive: just a gate in a cement wall with peeling, black paint. The gate opens into an outdoor corridor that leads past his cousin's house, and into a courtyard surrounding a dead tree in a large planter. A ferocious-looking, blue and brown eyed Akita greets us, barking her head off like she'd rather kill us than not. A one-bug-eyed pug with a perpetually protruding tongue happily accompanies her larger cohort in this bark-fest. Thankfully, the Akita whose name is, unfittingly, Chula, which means "cutie," is chained up so we're able to pass without being mauled.

The house is at the back of the courtyard. We go in and are greeted with a disaster: old furniture piled here and there, moldy looking walls with peeling paint, and a kitchen that looks like it was never finished. Yet, there's something about it. It has good bones, if you know what I mean: large windows at the front framed by adobe brick and wood beams, and a wide, tiled staircase with a wrought iron banister. Up the staircase is a central room, also with a wall of large windows through which the late afternoon light streams. There are two bedrooms off this main room, which could be a family room, or, I suppose, another bedroom if everyone in the household is very friendly with one another. I say this, in particular, because there are no doors in the doorways to the bedrooms—in fact, it appears there never were. Each bedroom has large, empty window frames that look into the family room. Also, the upstairs bathroom, one large space with no separation between the shower and the rest of the room, has no door on it. There are also no closets, though in one bedroom there's a big cabinet with a rod for hanging clothes. Downstairs, tucked behind a curved wall under the staircase is a half bath, which actually has a toilet seat on the toilet, though the one upstairs doesn't. That bathroom, however, also does not have a door, nor is there any possible way to add one. All the floors in the house are tile, and the walls are cement so the slightest sound—at this moment, the barking dog—echoes throughout the place.

Marco tells us this is where he lived with his young daughters and his wife until they got divorced three years ago. That's why he's let it go to pieces. He just couldn't stand to deal with it, he says. I'm thinking the divorce probably happened due to the complete and utter lack of privacy.

The interesting thing is, even though he was devastated by the divorce, he reveals that he was in a relationship after that with the Peace Corps worker who came to teach at the university. In a sense, I'm basically taking her place at the school. It was an affair that began before COVID, and which ended when the pandemic broke out. She had to leave, and left him with all her stuff: a fairly new mattress, sheets, towels, blankets and lots of clothes. Apparently, she had been living in one of those other apartments we saw, but he moved her stuff here since he was using it as a warehouse anyway. He expected her to return, but she never did. Poor guy. He suddenly takes on a sad, romantic aspect in my eyes.

Though we like the house on one level, it needs a ton of work before we can even move in. We technically have two more weeks reserved at the place in Mixquiahuala but we're itching to get out of there. Marco says that, if we want the place, he could get it cleaned out and cleaned up in a few days. That seems like a stretch, but we tell him we would be willing to do the work of plastering and painting, maybe adding a door or two and other repairs, and he says that he would take money off the rent for costs we incur. We haven't agreed on a rental price yet, but this is starting to feel like a possibility. Also, there's a big, new sofa in the downstairs living room, and a usable dining set in the dining room. This is a relatively big house and would be perfect for us, especially for hosting guests. There's also a huge, brand-new refrigerator in the kitchen and a beautiful stove. The kitchen sink, on the other hand, sits on a rusty metal stand between the fridge and stove, with virtually no counter top. What should be a counter, opposite the appliances, is an island between the kitchen and dining room topped with coarse cement and covered with a sheet of plastic. It's hard to fathom how much work this place is going to take.

We're not ready to come to a decision yet, so we run it by Rico, who has no real opinion about any of the places we've seen. I think he thinks we're crazy Americans to even be considering Marco's place, but he says it's up to us and he doesn't think we're crazy either way. Sure.

We sleep on it. In the morning, we decide we'll go see Marco's place one more time. We're feeling like it's the best option. We didn't get a good vibe from the landlord of the other apartments anyway.

So, we meet with Marco again at the house that afternoon. We look around again and, this time, go up the tiny spiral staircase to the roof where, ostensibly, one would hang their laundry to dry (though there's no washer in the house). There, with the breeze blowing, the sun shining, and a view of the distant hills, we tell Marco we'll take the place. I propose what I think will be a fair rent, based on what the other places we've seen are charging, and he agrees. I say we'll want to put some doors in, tile the kitchen counter, plaster, paint, etc., and he reiterates that he'll deduct it from the rent. We agree that whatever furniture we buy for the place, which is going to include a couple of beds, nightstands, coffee table, desk and chair for Jon to work at, etc., plus whatever else we put into the house like artwork, curtains, this, and that, we will leave for him. He will come out of it with a beautiful home to rent or sell in the future. We all love the idea and we shake on it. "*Trato hecho*," he says: "done deal." He says we can move in by Saturday. It's now Wednesday, and tomorrow, as I mentioned, is Independence Day. I can't imagine he'll work over the holiday, but he promises us Saturday it will be. And, he'll even come to get us and our stuff in Mixquiahuala. Beautiful.

We leave feeling excited and a little nervous. Is he really going to pull this off? If so, I'll just cancel the remaining ten days at the B&B, forfeiting the rest of the money as per the cancelation policy. I don't mind. The place is only about $20 a night, so, yeah, we'll lose $200 but it will be well worth it. The amount we'll be paying Marco for rent only equals about $150 a month American, so we feel like we're going to be ahead no matter what. I won't tell the owner of the B&B yet though. In fact, I won't tell her until we're out. She won't mind. She'll pocket the money, and can rent it out to someone else if she wants. Whoever they are, I pity them.

From Jon:

These are the people of the rebar forest

Homes in progress
Or abandoned long ago
Or occupied with family gathered
Aspiring always to greater elevation
Never finished
Even at completion
Lightening-rod gardens grace the rooftops
Competing in cooperation for the bright future
Out there
Over there
Evocative
Elusive
Almost within reach
A cat at arm's length
Smooth
Soft
Compelling
Calling for the touch
But maybe clawed

These are the people of kindness
Of buen día to passersby
Of warmth and laughter
Of tradition and structure
Drums and bugles
Signs held high
Of celebration

These are the people whose words for darling and sky are the same
The blue darling
The dearest above me
The ceiling corrugated

The lighting - bare bulbed

These are the sweet-toothed ones
Fruit and cream con azúcar
Corn and corn
Hot sweet tamales
Honey is Miel
Luna de Miel
It's not spicy if it only burns the tongue for a little while

Mansion and ramshackle
Peacefully side-by-side
Great art
Tiled visions of wonder
Cinderblock and tin roof
Home
Never homeless
Street-life an impossible admission

Dogs roam
Sleeping
Dreaming masters
Yet not-masters feed them
Water them
Clean after them
Not one goes without
Community perros

Woven together in real time
Brick and cement and rebar
Connections of necessity
Attraction
Desire

These are the people
Connected
Eyes lifted
To the future
To great things
To the rebar forests

200,000 to 350,000 Steps

By now you get the idea that we're walking, on average, at least 10,000 steps a day. This is not out of a desire to stay fit though that's a bonus; it's simply survival. Heck, I can get almost that just walking around the university though I'm still not officially teaching yet. Mostly, we get the steps walking up and down the main drag in Mixquiahuala, looking for stuff we need or just a restaurant that doesn't qualify as street food though Mixquiahuala doesn't have many more restaurants than San Agustín does.

The other problem with finding a place for dinner is that Mexicans eat on a different schedule than we do. They have a little something early in the morning, coffee and a sweet roll maybe, then a big breakfast between 9:00 and 11:00, then the main meal of the day around 2:00 or 3:00. Later in the evening, say around 8:00 or 9:00, they have supper, usually something light, or they grab a slice of pizza, a hotdog, or a crepe from a stand. They're big on crepes. But I have breakfast at home before I set off for the day, then a sandwich or salad or whatever for lunch, in the usual American way, and by 6:00 or so, we're ready for dinner. By that time most of the restaurants have closed. Therefore, if we want to eat out, we're either stuck grabbing something from the "food court," or heading to that one nice restaurant in San Agustín, La Hacienda, which, thankfully, is open all afternoon and into the evening.

Anyway, today is Independence Day and the school is having a party to celebrate. Rico says to be there by noon. Each department of the school, meaning English, Engineering, Finance, Computer Science, etc., is hosting their own luncheon, outdoors, under a big tent. To participate you pay a few pesos to partake in whatever it is your department is serving. The English department is serving up *pozole,* a type of soup made with hominy corn, a traditional dish of the season, with bread and dessert. Again, I'm worried about it being too spicy. It is, but I eat it anyway, throwing caution to the wind because it's delicious. Manuel, who is an English teacher but associates with the Agricultural department, invites me to share their offering, *barbacoa*. Do NOT think this means barbeque in the American sense. It's mutton, wood roasted in a pit in the ground, then served in a tortilla like a taco. Somewhere along the way, someone has taken this roasted sheep from the pit and transferred it to a bin lined with a trash bag. I look into the bin to see the cooked meat with the sheep's head, eyeballs, horns and all, staring up at me. I almost balk. Is this considered street food? But it's too late to back down now and it would be very rude to refuse it. *Barbacoa* is the specialty in this region of Hidalgo, a delicacy, in fact, only prepared for special occasions. So, I take the tortilla full of the mutton that Manuel hands me and take a bite. It's delicious. I now pray it won't kill me.

At the celebration there are traditional dancers in their beautiful costumes and lots of music. There are also speeches, because these are obligatory, and a general air of revelry. Jon has come to the university with me and we're both happy to have been made a part of it. We're also feeling relieved that tomorrow is our last full day in Mixquiahuala.

We drop by the house after the celebration to see what progress Marco has made, which is very little. Is this really going to happen in two days' time? He says yes, no problem.

Friday is a day off for most people but Marco has kept his word and gotten most of the junk out that he's been storing in the house. It still hasn't been cleaned, though. He'll do that tomorrow morning, he says.

Come Saturday morning, we get our stuff packed up. Marco says he'll come get us at 3:00. After we take one last walk through Mixquihuala, we have nothing else to do but sit in the smelly apartment and wait. Three o'clock comes and goes. He's on his way, he says, but got delayed and will be there at 4:00. Just before 4:00 we haul our stuff and, of course, the cat, downstairs and wait in the smelly hallway with the door propped open. Finally, about 4:30, he arrives in his Cadillac SUV, with his petite, and very young girlfriend in the front seat. In fact, we're not sure if it's his daughter or his girlfriend. All we know is she's a waitress at his café. He seems appalled at the quantity of stuff we have, but we manage to cram it in the SUV, and merrily go on to our new house.

When we get there, he seems proud to show it off but my heart sinks at the work that still needs to be done. Also, I'd hardly call it clean. Yet, as far as he's concerned, he's done all he's going to do for now, so he leaves us to it. I get to mopping the floors, only to find out that the white tile is stained with the red grout and it will not come out no matter what. It looks really bad. Also, upstairs, there are several loose tiles in the floors, and the lights don't work in one of the bedrooms. We lay out the mattress that had belonged to his girlfriend in the other bedroom, and make the bed with sheets she'd left and which we'd washed at the Air B and B. I was counting on Marco leaving some pillows that had been there in a bag, but the bag is gone. We have no pillows. I text him to ask him about it and he said his mother has taken them to wash. That's nice, but we have no pillows.

So, I take the vinyl pillow covers off of the couch pillows and put regular pillow cases on them. They're lumpy and uncomfortable but they'll have to do for now. We go to have dinner at La Hacienda because it's right around the corner and we need some comfort right about now. We're clearly going to be roughing it until we can get this place pulled together.

What we have for furniture is the mattress on the floor of our bedroom, a large, ugly cabinet where we can put our clothes, the sectional couch in the living room, which someone has thankfully cleaned and at least is fairly comfortable, a dining room table that wobbles, eight chairs some of which are missing decorative parts, a dish cabinet with no glass in the windows and no knobs on the cupboards, the nice, stainless steel fridge, the stove, which, like the one in the house at the school, is not connected to gas (though, to be fair, they did finally get the stove in the campus house connected after five days). We're back to having no dishes, silverware, cups, glasses, or pots and pans. Marco says to drop by the café to borrow some cookware he has lying around. It's not much or fancy, but it's a start.

Sunday, gratefully, is *tianguis* day, and so we gather some necessities and some food for the house, including some pretty Talavera pottery cups, plates and bowls. It's going to take a lot to get this place together. At least I have my extra half-bathroom, even if it doesn't have a door.

From Jon: One of my first tasks after we moved in was to march myself over to a huge hardware store just down the block to get a toilet seat. Strangely enough (to me anyway) they didn't carry them. Not enough demand? I have no idea. The good thing is that there are lots of smaller hardware stores scattered around town. Somehow, they don't exactly compete because they all carry different hardware. That's a guess. The next store actually had some on display, but the ones they had wouldn't fit on our newer, more modern, toilet. I did have to bring Geo back to the store with me to make sure I was understanding correctly. They had toilet seats only for toilets that were at least thirty years old. I suppose I should not have been surprised but I was. Still, the very friendly owner said he'd order one, and we could expect it by next Thursday. All our communication until I brought Geo in was pretty much sign language, but somehow, we managed well enough—up to a point. Right. So, I went back bright-and-early the next Thursday morning, and was told to come back after 4:00. The words americano loco *were not uttered aloud, but I had the feeling. It wasn't mean or anything, rather an unspoken observation. I still did not know the way things worked in San Agustín. Anyway, I made the purchase, brought it home, installed it and, naturally, less than a week later, the other toilet seat broke. I went back to the same hardware store to buy another one. The guy told me to come back on Thursday. Newer toilet seats are so rare it appears they can only be purchased by special order. These things are like unicorns. I'm learning.*

We've been dreading going to the immigration office in Pachuca but there's no more putting it off. Even though COMEXUS has been very clear about what to bring, the ETAs who have already done it report varying experiences in the offices in their states, and that making an appointment is impossible. You just show up and hope for the best.

Jon and I dutifully catch the bus at 9:00 a.m. in San Agustín, and it lurches along, arriving in Pachuca at about 10:15. By the time the driver shoos us off the bus, telling us this is the closest stop to the immigration office, I have to pee like a mo———-. Well, let's just say I *really* need to pee. We start walking with no idea where we're going. Pachuca is a big city, the capital of Hidalgo. By this point, Jon has gotten his portable hotspot to work, but the directions it gives us to the immigration office are no help at all because in order to go where it says to go, we'd have to cross major highways. Anyway, I'm not going to make it walking because my bladder is about to burst. We pass a couple of official looking buildings that I hope may have a bathroom, but I'm too shy to ask.

We've been told not to hail a cab in major cities, especially Mexico City but, for safety reasons, to call an Uber instead. Well, Uber doesn't exist in Pachuca, nor does Lyft. It's a big city but not that big. So, left to no other choice, we hail a passing cab. The driver is perfectly nice and gets us to the immigration office in about 10 minutes. Thank God they have a bathroom. That was a close one.

We sign in and sit in the waiting room with our masks on. We would not have been allowed into the building without them. I don't think I've mentioned that the state of Hidalgo is still under a mask mandate for COVID though that's not the case in every state in Mexico. We wear them dutifully, including when I'm at school, but we've noticed that when people get together, like at Rico's parents' house or the school Independence Day festival, there's nary a mask in sight.

I believe I have all our papers in order but, when the severe-looking woman calls us up to the window, she glares at them and sighs. We're missing certain documents, and copies of others, she tells us. We'll have to come back in three days. She gives us an appointment for 2:20 in the afternoon, just 40 minutes before they close for that day, and hands me a printed sheet with everything circled in red that I need to bring.

Dejected, we get a taxi to the *Central de Autobus* and head home. The bus ride is long and hot. To make matters worse, a clown gets on in Actopan—yes, an actual clown with red nose attached, cheeks painted, and floppy red shoes—and proceeds to "entertain" us, his literally captive audience, with bad joke after bad joke until he ends his set with a long, long, maudlin song, via DVD player, about a son who never appreciated his deceased mother. Will the torture never end?

These trips to Pachuca mean I have to take days off from teaching but, fortunately, Rico is agreeable to it. He kind of has to be. If I don't get this taken care of by the end of the month, I will actually be deported. And we are now into the third week of September.

Thursday, we catch the bus in San Agustín at 12:30, get to the *Central* (terminal) in Pachuca, which we now know is the best place to get a taxi (and they have bathrooms) by 1:45. We are at the immigration office by 2:00. The lady calls us up before our appointment time, but she's still unsatisfied with our documents. She says to me in Spanish "No, you need copies of this one and this one, and you haven't filled out this form online. You'll need to go to the internet café down the street and take care of it."

Crap! Finding that particular form on their website is ridiculously hard. I thought I'd filled it out before but, apparently, it didn't save. Freaking out, my heart pounding, Jon and I haul our butts up the street to the café. I plunk down at a computer, and manage to get to the site. Somehow, and to this day I don't know how, I do it: I find the form. I get it filled out, hands shaking, print out the documents, and ask the guy at the counter to copy them for me, which he does with great haste. The whole thing has taken about 15 minutes and it's now 2:30. We run back to the office and the lady looks over our stuff again. We did it! She doesn't seem nearly as thrilled about our success as we do, but I suppose bureaucrats are what they are world-wide. It's all there. Now, it's picture taking time. She photographs us, resulting in the most horrific pictures either Jon or I have ever taken, gives us *temporary* documents, and then gives us an appointment to come back next week to get the *official* cards. What?!?! We have to come back again?

Incredulous, we catch another taxi, and hop another bus back to San Agustín. We are again regaled with the entertainment stylings of the clown.

My temporary resident card is enough to satisfy the bank lady at least, so now I'm able to take care of that situation, after, of course, another two hours waiting in the bank. It should be noted that the bank has a rule that the guards enforce with pomp and circumstance: no phones, tablets, or computers are allowed to be used while waiting in the bank for service. Those of us in line share a word or two, but mostly spend our time staring blankly at the splendor of the bank walls.

I'm finally able to breathe a sigh of relief. We won't be deported, and I'll be paid on time.

From Jon: On the second trip to San Agustín from Pachuca on the bus, on the left side, there's a hill that looks like a gigantic breast from a certain angle. I thought, oh, I have to get a photo of it for my nephew, who will appreciate it. I couldn't get it, but, on the third trip back, I positioned myself on that side of the bus, my camera ready. As we got to the perfect spot, a truck lodged itself between us and the bus, and never moved until the shot was lost. It took me until just a few weeks before the end of our stay in Mexico before I finally got the shot. There's nothing quite like a hill shaped like a breast.

350,000 to 500,000 Steps

With only one more trip to Pachuca on my schedule, I am finally able to dig in to the teaching. Though my title is English Teaching Assistant, Rico refers to me as a co-teacher, and that is my job. I am not supposed to be an assistant in the sense of that I help the other teacher to teach their lessons, necessarily. I am supposed to be prepared with activities of my own and, while I present them, the teacher that I'm working with in that given classroom is supposed to support me, work with me, and teach with me. Then, when they have an activity or a lesson to present, I am to do the same for them. Somehow this memo hasn't entirely gotten out to the teachers though they've all been working with ETAs, from Fulbright or Peace Corps, for years.

My first day with any given teacher usually consists of me doing a Q and A session with the group, as a kind of cultural introduction. Each student writes a question for me in English, the other teacher and I go around and check that the questions are written correctly, then each student in turn asks me the question in front of the class, and I answer it. I tell them they can ask me anything they want except my age. This activity always goes well. It's fun, the students are engaged, and I'm quipping with them—all of us having a good time.

The first time I work with Manuel, we do this activity and then I participate as he gives his lesson: correcting pronunciation, checking the students' work, or presenting grammar, as Manuel wishes. He's the ideal teacher to work with in that we truly co-teach every moment. The two hours of his class are a little exhausting, though, as there's no down time.

The first time I work with Adela, a wanna-be actress (yes, they have them even in the wilds of Mexico), it goes fine but, the next time, she essentially ditches me. Her son is there at work with her and he's sick. Not COVID, she says, but she has to take him to the doctor. Do I mind running the class while she goes? What can I say? I don't want to be a jerk. So, I agree and do my activity while she takes off and never comes back. I dismiss the class early because it's not my job to entertain them in her absence and I have no idea what her lesson plan is.

The second time I am to "work" with her, she texts me ahead of time to let me know she has to go to a conference and, can I take over for her? I text her back that, according to my contract, I'm not allowed to sub for the teacher. It's co-teaching or nothing. She says she understands and so I tell the class what to work on in her absence and leave, quite angry, in fact.

The first time I work with a teacher named Irene, I get hopelessly lost trying to find her classroom. The two big, modern buildings on the campus, about a quarter of a mile from each other are called Docencia 1 and Docencia 2. Around 1,000 steps in another direction are buildings that are lettered L M N and O. Building O is where Manuel teaches, and Adela is in building M, which has four classrooms on each side of the building, downstairs and up. However, they are not actually marked with the numbers 1-4, rather with the number of the group that meets there—like AG15S—which means nothing to me.

At this point, these are all the buildings I'm aware of. When Irene tells me she's in Building D, room 2, I'm really baffled. I go wandering around the LMNO buildings, figuring the alphabet must continue somewhere around there. There are, indeed, another group of buildings nearby, but they're fenced off. I've come to refer to that area as the Communist university, because it's a totally different school, on the same campus, with huge murals of Communist icons painted on the side: Marx, Lenin, Tolstoy, and...Stalin. Stalin? Really?

There's yet another university on the campus as well, the original one, in fact, built around 1920 in the revolution-era style of architecture. This, I learn, is called El Mexe, *mexe* (pronounced MEH-sheh) meaning spider in the indigenous language of the region, *hñähñu* (pronounced NYA-nyu). It was, until about ten years ago, what they call a *"Normal"* school, meaning a place where teachers teach teachers to teach. It then transformed into a regular university, but they've been on strike since the pandemic started, complaining mostly about having to hold virtual classes. I'm sure that's not all, but the people I've asked about it don't seem to really know what they are on strike about—they're just kind of always on strike. Around El Mexe are a variety of Communist banners, my favorite of which, sporting a hammer and sickle, and a spider symbol, bears the message: *"El peor enemigo de la revolución es el burgués que varios revolucionarios llevan al dentro,"* which means, roughly, "The worst enemy of the revolution is the bourgeois which some revolutionaries carry within."

Okay, so I'm still looking for building D. I text Irene, but it takes a while for her to text me back because, wherever she is, the wi-fi is not reliable. I go sit at one of the cement tables in front of what I think of as the cafeteria to wait. Finally she texts, "It's in front of the cafeteria." I swear I've looked at every building in the vicinity of the cafeteria and no building D. I say, "I can't find it." She sends me a picture of the building with a D on the side. Sigh. This means nothing to me. I see no building with a D on the side. I finally go ask Rico where building D is, but he doesn't seem to know. He calls Irene, and she gives him directions. He points me toward the direction of El Mexe, which is about 1,000 steps from the English office, across that same smelly canal that runs through Los Filtros, and in front of the OTHER cafeteria, which I did not know existed.

So, off I go, about 45 minutes late at this point but, I figure, that's not my fault. After I cross the canal, and wander through a wooded area, toward a cluster of low, long buildings, Irene comes running out and waves me toward her. As it turns out, she is a delight to work with but, like everyone on the campus, including Rico, seems to think I already know my way around though no one has given me a tour or, for that matter, a map. One thing I learn about teaching at this end of the campus is that there is a bathroom with toilet seats on the toilets—the only one on campus.

Today is the day to get our ID cards. I take another day off from school, and Jon and I get the bus in time to be in Pachuca for our appointment. It's not like we're not fascinated by the view from the bus. Even though it passes through a lot of scruffy little towns, to me, it's Mexico, and everything in Mexico is interesting. I've already mentioned the beautiful landscape between Actopan and Pachuca, and I never get tired of it.

My heart is pounding when we get to the office and go up to the window because I'm sure the lady will find some reason to deny us our cards. But no, she hands them to us, we sign some more stuff, and we're free. Free, and legal in Mexico. Breathing a huge sigh of relief, we take a taxi back to the bus station and clamber on board. Let me mention at this point that we've been very careful to wear masks on the buses, on the combis, in all crowded areas, at school, etc., but, by this time, we're so tired of that one hour and fifteen-minute ride stifled behind a mask, we take them off. The bus isn't too crowded and the windows are open, so we figure we're good. This time, we're spared the clown but, in his place, a young aspiring singer gets on with a karaoke machine and serenades the passengers very enthusiastically, and very off key.

The other passengers on the bus seem to endure the entertainment stoically, even though many of them are trying to sleep. I've taken to out-and-out, ineffectively, glaring at the clown, and now this joker too. I mean, come on! This concert lasts a solid half an hour until he finally gets off somewhere. I'm sure his mother is very proud of his talent and his ingenuity.

To be fair, in spite of how annoying these distractions are, people in this part of Mexico use whatever they have: selling home-made products like cookies, health-bars, *pan dulce*, tamales and the like, and performing: telling bad jokes, playing maudlin songs, or singing karaoke loudly and badly but with absolute confidence in order to survive.

Everybody in the poor to middle classes works. They work hard and constantly. As a result of this work ethic, these are some of the most industrious and creative people to be found anywhere.

From Jon:

I dream of Mexico upon awakening
Vibrante! Buen día!
Alive in pride, poverty, and riches
I am drawn to her
To sit in the warmth of her vision
Witnessing history
Moment everlasting
Time a concept
Nothing more
A future of fortune
Her song cries
Belleza! I am here!
Yo estoy aquí! Beauty!
Heart on display
On the street
In the marketplace
The work
Dawn beyond dusk,

On into the night
Always in progress
She too is awakening, dreaming
Of her people holding their breath
Holding her breath
Eyes open, ancho!
Wide!
Crinkled in laughter, love, and spice, hot...
Picante!
Love of family, friends,
America!
Love of rough-edged community
Love of shine, contrast, and color
Brillante!
Love of life in art in lives of art.
Mexico dreams me
Dreaming Mexico
Arms spread wide, welcoming
Always welcoming
All comers
Into the dream

500,000 Steps and Holding

We have COVID. So much for our daring mask removal on the bus. We're positive that's where we contracted it. That bus is nothing if not germy. It's the end of September, going on October, and we've been stuck in the house for a week. The first day, I didn't feel too bad, but Jon was incapacitated, so I went out for supplies. The next two days we were both flat in bed, staying alive with crackers and soup and whatnot. Rico offered to bring us whatever we needed, but I wouldn't have him risk it.

One thing I forgot to mention is that, while I've been at school, Marco and Jon have been fixing the loose tiles in the upstairs part of the house. Just before we realized we had COVID, Jon was working in close proximity to Marco, coughing a lot.

So, once we tested positive, I texted Marco to tell him and, low and behold, he has it too. Fortunately, we are all vaccinated, or at least as much as we can be since the latest round of boosters didn't come out before we left. All the Mexicans we've spoken to are vaccinated and boosted too, though the vaccine is not so easy to acquire in this part of the country. There is also a certain hesitancy amongst some people here (and it must be said, in the U.S. as well). At this point in 2022, about 60% of Mexicans are vaccinated, mostly the people who are a little better off. We are incredibly glad to be among the people who have embraced the science. Being sicker is unthinkable.

I feel bad that Marco has gotten it, but he quarantines, isolating himself from his family and is all right in about five days. It takes Jon and I that whole week to recover. As he starts to get better, I've got a sore throat that feels like fire, so then it's his turn to go get supplies.

You may be wondering at this point if we're still sleeping on a mattress on the floor. I'm happy to report we are not but getting a bed was a real situation. First of all, just a few days after we moved in mid-September, and amidst the rigamarole with the immigration office, we took a combi to Progreso to the one department store they have there, called Coppel. We looked around at beds, testing them out, with a nice lady helping us. They were pretty expensive, but we finally settled on a queen that seemed relatively comfortable, and was fairly reasonable. It came with a box spring and a base with legs. Nothing fancy, but it was all we needed. Once we decided on the bed, she led us down to the cashier, where we would pay and arrange for the delivery. That whole process seemed unnecessarily complicated, but I carefully iterated our address for the guy and we agreed on a date. The bed would arrive in two days.

When delivery day came, the bed did not. Because of another complicated situation with my Mexican phone sim card, I couldn't call Coppel to find out what happened. Marco very sweetly offered to drive Jon back to the store to straighten it out. Marco is a lawyer for the local mine so we felt it was good to have him on our side. Anyway, at the store, Jon and Marco were informed that the mattress had been delivered to an address in Michoacan, a completely different state six hours away! Why would we order a bed in Hidalgo, to be delivered to Michoacan? The guy showed Jon the address but, as it turns out, there are tons of San Agustíns in Mexico. I guess he'd decided that one was as good as another.

The guy was loathe to take responsibility for the error, but apparently Marco "convinced" him to fix it and he did. A day later, the bed was delivered. It was not what we ordered—a king sized bed of a different brand altogether, and rather hard. Once assembled, it nearly filled the space in the room from wall to wall but we were not about to send it back.

We waited for the delivery guys to set it up and then we went out to find sheets. We looked in every likely store in town, but requests for king-sized sheets drew blank stares. I imagine they considered sheets for a king-sized bed something only movie stars would be asking for. We finally wandered into a tiny store that sells all kinds of unexpected things from capers to suitcases and, sure enough, they had them, and they turned out to be very high quality.

We had also acquired a few other pieces of furniture by the time we went down with COVID, including a saloon-type door for the upstairs bathroom that a carpenter made for us (don't ask why we went for that kind of door—it seemed like a good idea at the time), a beautifully crafted coffee table, made by a different carpenter, a wool blanket that served as a living room rug, a desk built by yet another local carpenter, an office chair for Jon, some old curtains that we'd found in the house and had dry cleaned, and blankets for our bed. Blankets are not so easy to find in San Agustín, but you can hunt them down—pillows not at all—and we never could get Marco to bring us back the pillows he took. He did, however, help Jon round up some industrial cleaning solution for the floor tiles to get rid of the stains. Jon and I scrubbed the crap out of the floor with that noxious smelling, Pepto-Bismol-pink solution that produced a suspicious unmoving cloud of vapor. We could literally see it hanging in the air of the room. Either that, or our vision had become severely blurred. In either case, we made ourselves scarce upstairs. The vendor had insisted when Jon bought it that the stuff was completely organic, safe, and non-toxic. Possibly that was true for some other organic, possibly silicone-based, life forms but not for the two of us, nor the cat. The floor did look better though. As that old SNL line goes, "It's better to look good than to feel good."

We had also ordered a tiny espresso maker for Jon, and we purchased an air fryer at a local furniture store. It was a strange place that offered absolutely ugly overpriced furniture, and a few reasonably priced small appliances. We chose the air fryer over a microwave, reasoning that it would be much more useful to us. Turned out to be a very good choice. When we wanted hot water, we also now had gas (propane) hooked up to the stove. Yes! We were becoming relatively, U.S. style, comfortable. We still foresaw another couple of months of repairs and decorating, but it was getting there. You might also ask why we were investing all this time and money in a house we were only going to be living in for nine months. Well, first of all, remember that Marco was paying for the permanent improvements by means of us deducting money from the rent each month. But, as far as the furniture and home décor went, it was important for us that the house not only be comfortable for those nine months, but beautiful as well. As I mentioned, the house already had a lot of nice features, it had just been sorely neglected. Jon had also been working on the plastering that was needed in various areas of the house, and I had been in charge of painting over it with what passed as paint, but was actually whitewash.

Also, we thought of the house as something of an art project that would ultimately be a gift to Marco. Jon is a sculptor and a painter and he has imbued every house we've lived in with his own art and vision. The interesting thing about this house was that, because we didn't want to spend more than we had to make it beautiful and livable, we ended up using items we found at the *tianguis* and around town, using those things in ways other than their intended use. For instance, as is common in many of the homes here, the house had a lot of bare light bulbs hanging from the ceilings. Light fixtures would have been the obvious choice to cover them up, but we couldn't find any in San Agustín, and ordering them would have been expensive. So Jon found some small baskets for about twenty pesos (about a dollar) each at the *tianguis* that would just fit over a lightbulb. Since the bulbs were the LED kind that didn't get hot, he attached the baskets to the base of the bulb with wire, and they turned out to be really effective. They hid the bulb, and softened the light. Everyone who came into the house after that, Mexican or not, and noticed the baskets, were amazed at how great they looked. The general attitude was, "Why hasn't anyone thought of that before?"

I mentioned we were paying the equivalent of $150 dollars a month in rent. In Mexico, that's a lot of money: about $3000 pesos. But, for us, it was a pretty reasonable percentage of my monthly payment from COMEXUS, and our income was also supplemented by rent we were receiving for our house in Portland, some money from the Air B and B that we have in the lower part of that house, money Jon made for classes he taught at an online university, and other income from some online consulting. Of course, we also had ongoing bills in Portland that needed to be paid, but this money covered all that easily with something left over for us to use for things in Mexico above and beyond what COMEXUS had estimated we would need. When we figured out how much we were spending on furniture and other improvements to the house (that Marco didn't cover), plus the rent, and divided it among nine months, the total came out to about $300 a month. I'm sorry, but where in the world can you live for $300 a month? Granted, San Agustín is one of the least expensive towns in Mexico; food is cheap (for us, anyway), transportation is cheap, and other necessities are too. What we needed and couldn't get we either ordered from Amazon Mexico, regular Amazon if that item was not available from AMX, or simply did without. Our day-to-day expenses in Mexico were far, far cheaper than they were in Portland—which is why, I suppose, Americans choose to go to Mexico to live, I mean, besides the fact that it's an amazing place to be.

This brings me to want to describe more about San Agustín, and why, sick in bed with COVID, I'm resentful that I can't go out wandering around the town as Jon and I have gotten used to doing, whether to get groceries or other necessities, or to just explore. As small as the town is, it seems like there's always more to explore.

The main part of the town is the *centro* or plaza. It sits directly across the street from the church, something very typical of Mexican towns, because, of course, when the towns were first built (or colonized) by the Spaniards, the churches were meant to be the center of everything. As I previously pointed out, San Agustín has a very pretty, and quite large church, in the Spanish colonial style, with a soaring bell tower. The bell, which tolls every quarter hour, has become part of the background of everyday life here for us.

The plaza area has probably been expanded since the early days of the town. On one side is a basketball court that becomes an event space when there is something special going on—often every weekend. In the center of the plaza is a fountain, and surrounding it, an open area with benches where people can gather, a gazebo, and fenced in areas of grass, shrubs, and cactus. On the northwest side of the plaza is the daily marketplace, a building in the revolution-era style, built in 1941, kind of a lovely mix of Art Deco and colonial architecture. It's being renovated now so the venders sell their fruits, vegetables, and meats under a large tent just in front of the building. The town officials probably moved everyone outside when the pandemic hit and then decided it was a good excuse to renovate. I love the daily market—the whole idea of going every day to get the fresh things you need to make dinner—and I quickly made friends with the vendors. So did Jon since he's often the one in charge of the shopping. Even with his limited Spanish, he manages quite well and they love him.

Across from the marketplace, on the northeast side of the plaza, is the food court, which I've talked about before. I don't think it's called a food court in Spanish but I don't know what else to call it. In the morning, people are at their stands, preparing mostly *gorditas*, the iconic food of San Agustín. It's kind of like a thick corn tortilla stuffed with meat: chicken, beef, or various animal body parts, like a cross between a taco and a pita. They are a popular breakfast item. You can either go inside and sit and eat at communal tables, or on stools at windows on the street side. At 3:00 in the afternoon, the gordita stalls close, and some of them are taken over by people making and selling *tacos dorados* (what we might think of as *taquitos*) and street style tacos. Jon and I have fallen in love with those *tacos dorados* but try not to eat them that often, since they're fried after all. You can also get sublime roast chicken at one of the food court windows, and at various other stands around San Agustín.

All around the plaza are little shops, all with the same style of carved wooden signs hanging in front, which gives the town center a nice feeling of continuity. Though San Agustín has a slightly run-down quality, it also has a great deal of charm. What's more important is that the people are incredibly warm, which has totally endeared it to us. We love this place, truly love it.

There are many more blocks of shops in streets that form a grid radiating out from the center for a few hundred yards in every direction, and then the neighborhoods begin, houses that are mostly connected to each other along the streets. All of it is interesting to explore, but it's really the *centro* that is the heart and soul of San Agustín. It is also the heart and soul of all of its celebrations, and we're looking forward to many of those during the upcoming holidays, when, for sure, we'll be past this stupid virus and with extra immunities to spare!

From Jon: I had come to realize by this point that in all of San Agustín and surrounding it, I would be hard pressed to find a decent cup of coffee. While this was strange in the extreme to me, as Mexico is a coffee growing country, most restaurants and "coffee" shops were openly proud to offer something called Nescafe. *The only way I have to describe this instant concoction is, well, disgusting. Marco's café did manage to brew a decent cup, and even made a pretty good mocha but it had cow milk not almond, and (what I thought at the time) straight-up sugar. Also, his hours of operation had a lot to do with how he felt about opening on any given day. I like a nice almond-milk mocha with agave nectar, first thing. With that in mind, I decided to see if Amazon could deliver to our little, out of the way, town. To my delight they indicated that they could. I ordered a small, inexpensive cappuccino maker.*

I searched several local markets and finally discovered one that actually sold ground coffee (from Columbia). I located a different store that sold cacao (this is the unprocessed version of cocoa—meaning that it is nutritionally superior, though more of it has to be used to get the right flavor). I also found agave syrup in the same store. Why these items are difficult to find in their country of origin is baffling to me to this day.

I waited for the delivery of the cappuccino maker. I even arranged with Marco, so that if they came to deliver when I was not home, they could drop it at the café—if it happened to be open. I waited some more. Weeks passed. I looked at the tracker and found that it had been stuck in Pachuca for more than a week. I wrote to customer service and they declared the item lost, and returned my money. I bravely reordered, and a week later my little cappuccino machine arrived. The next morning, I was a happy imbiber of exactly the concoction I wanted. Three days after that, the "lost" item was delivered. I once again contacted customer service to let them know, and to see how they wanted it to be returned. They told me to keep it, knowing full well that, no matter what, it was unlikely to ever actually arrive back in the U.S., let alone to the Amazon warehouse. I gifted it to Marco. The bottom line for me was that Amazon could deliver. It took me a while longer to discover Amazon Mexico. They could deliver also. All the things that were completely unavailable within a reasonable distance from town we could have delivered with a pretty reasonable expectation of receiving it. Cool. Amazon is not my favorite company on the planet, but in that time of necessity they represented the mother of invention.

500,000 to 650,000 Steps

It's mid-October. We've recovered from COVID though we've both still got a bit of a cough. I returned to school last week but my energy was low. Still, last night we went to Marco's birthday party at his parents' house, where I guess he also lives. We didn't know what to bring as a gift so I brought flowers to his mother, Maria. She and Marco's father, Fernando, are amazing people. She is a professional baker, though she used to be a teacher, and he is a retired Spanish teacher who worked at El Mexe when it was a *"Normal."* Like many people in San Agustín, they are a highly educated family and conversing with them is really interesting because they know so much about a variety of topics. It's also a great for my Spanish practice because they don't speak English.

In spite of everyone being friendly and welcoming, we felt a little out of place at the party because we don't really know anyone but the family, but the food was delicious: chicken with a tomato-y sauce steamed in foil, which apparently is really popular at parties here, and pork in *mole* (pronounced MOH-lay, a sauce, often cacao based), with rice, all made by Maria, who is serving about thirty people. The main attraction was the cake though, a chocolate cake, made, of course, by Maria, and which Jon was dying for. I don't eat cake, generally, because I avoid sugar, but the small taste I had told me it was bliss.

This afternoon, we've got another event on our social calendar. I've gotten to know a young guy from my university named Arlo when he came to the English chat sessions I offer. He let me know he was gay at our second meeting by casually mentioning his boyfriend. I was astonished that in a small, rural place like San Agustín, people are so open and accepting of his sexual orientation, but apparently they are—and of trans people too, he informed me.

He texted me yesterday to ask if Jon and I would like to go to a party with him today. He says it will be a typical Mexican party, which sounds great, and the kind of experience we crave. I ask about what to wear, and he informs me that it will basically be a party in a cornfield outside of town. So, jeans? Yes, definitely. Very casual.

I'm imagining pick-up trucks and cowboy boots, loud music either of the *cumbia*, *banda*, *ranchero*, *norteño*, or American rock and roll variety, *barbacoa* tacos and other kinds of sloppy foods. In fact, that's the first thing I ask him: "Will there be food?"

"Lots of it," he replies.

So, Jon and I both dress in jeans and T-shirts. I wear my Prince "Purple Rain," t-shirt, and Jon's is wearing The Killers shirt he got at the concert we went to a week before we left for Mexico. Both of us wear sneakers, because I figure, "corn fields."

We meet Arlo and his boyfriend Fabricio in the center of town near the taxi stand. Arlo has a car, and he'll be driving us to this far-flung place. As soon as I see them, I know there's something amiss. They are both wearing nice slacks, button-down shirts, fancy boots, and smell of cologne. Arlo is dangling a gift bag from his finger.

"What kind of party is this again?" I ask him.

"It's a baptism party."

"What? But you said it was casual. You said it was in a cornfield!"

"It is, it is!" he assures me. "Everyone is very casual in Mexico. And besides, you're Americans. They expect you to be casual."

This doesn't sit well with me at all. They *expect* us to be casual? I interpret this to mean that we're going to look like stupid foreigners without a clue about how to dress or behave at a nice party. "And what about a gift? Shouldn't we bring one too?"

"No, no, no. You're my guest. You don't have to bring a gift."

This situation seems to be going south very fast. We're going to show up, underdressed, with no gift, at a baptism celebration for the child of people we don't know at all.

I decide to take Arlo at his word. Maybe everyone will be dressed casually. He's not, Fabricio's not, but, hopefully, everyone else will be.

We drive to the outskirts of town and beyond. Past the university, along a dirt road and the smelly canal, getting lost more than once, until finally we arrive at, essentially, a hacienda. Ok, sure, there are cornfields all around this enormous compound, but it's far from "in a cornfield." The people going in are dressed to the nines.

Inside, I see lamé, sequins, and gauzy fabrics draped on every female. The men are a bit more casual, in their Mexican embroidered shirts and nice jeans. Cowboy boots and hats abound. Yet, no one is more casual than we are. I'm mortified. I have a couple of perfectly nice dresses I could have worn, and Jon could have at least put on a shirt with buttons. He doesn't seem fazed, but I'm a little irked. If I can't depend on my gay friend to tell me the right thing to wear, who can I depend on?

We take seats at a table with four available places. The tables are laid with linen tablecloths, napkins, and flower centerpieces, and the tent that covers the enormous grass-covered yard of this gorgeous home is filled with balloons and other baby-oriented decorations. As soon as we sit down, we're served rice and chicken *mole*. After that comes fresh tortillas, pork *carnitas* and salsa, and then the highlight of the dinner, *barbacoa*. I have to admit that I'm not quite as enamored of the *barbacoa* as most *hidalguenses* (people from Hidalgo). Mutton has never been my favorite though this has a beautiful wood-roasted flavor, and they tend to serve the cuts with the most fat on them, which these people of Hidalgo covet. If they can get to the fat before everyone else, they go for it, particularly the old men who reach in, using their tortillas, and grab that fat!

The proud mother and father sit with the baby, clad in purest white and lace. She is a treasure: a tiny, sweet girl who doesn't cry once though out this entire soiree, and who poses in all her adorable splendor for every photo taken of her—which are a lot.

As we eat the delicious food, we chat amiably with Arlo and Fabricio until the band starts up. They both dance with various women friends of theirs. It is in between one of these numbers that I ask Arlo if it is acceptable for him and Fabricio to dance together. He says it is, and they have, but since both of them only know how to lead, dancing together is kind of a mess. This is a much more practical answer than I expected. So, then I pry further, genuinely interested in the level of tolerance and inclusion the small rural town of San Agustín offers these two lovely young men. Arlo says their sexual orientation is no problem in this place. People accept them, and all gay people, no problem (though to tell you the truth, I haven't noticed any other gay male couples in town, though maybe a few female). I'm truly impressed by this, and think, *good for San Agustín*! It being a very Catholic *pueblo*, as most are in Mexico, this is surprising to me. Arlo attributes part of this open-mindedness to the priest of the church, whom he refers to as "trans" because he dresses as the Virgin Mary every Christmas. So cool. He says it's also because this is a town of teachers, who tend to have a more progressive view of things.

Jon and I dance once or twice though it's hard to wow the crowd with our swing dancing skills (we took classes for about four years—several years ago) since the dance floor is made of grass. Also, I'm still embarrassed that I'm wearing non-party clothes.

All in all, though, the party is a blast. The band is straight up *norteño*—not my music of choice but I like the spirit of it—and the people love it. We meet friends of Arlo's, many of whom speak English impeccably, and we end up feeling comfortable and accepted—because, after all, this is Mexico. Welcoming strangers into their midst and the very literal "my house is your house" attitude is their vibe. This is something we experience every day and we appreciate it to no end.

We leave the party with Arlo and Fabricio on the early side because they have another party to go to, which of course they invite us to. We decline. We've partied enough. Arlo tells us this is how he operates, scheduling several events in one night so he can see all his friends and optimize his social time (and so he can have cake everywhere he goes—he loves cake). It's one of the many delightful qualities he possesses.

Speaking of Jon's Killers t-shirt, he absolutely treasures it. That concert was one we had bought tickets to a year before—while the pandemic was still raging—as a sign of hope that all would be well by the time the concert date finally arrived. In fact, we bought them before I had even applied for the Fulbright though, once I did, we kept our fingers crossed that, if I was accepted, we wouldn't be sent to Mexico before August 22nd of 2022. As luck would have it, we still had that week's window, and we went to the concert as high on life, excitement, and possibly other substances as we could be. The concert was epic and it was there I purchased the t-shirt for Jon. I tell you this for a reason.

We are desperate to find a good solution to getting our laundry done. The place we took our clothes that first week we were in town, where they did such a great job, is far from us—down by the university. I still have the number of that person, whose name is Ambar, and so I text to ask her if they can pick up and drop off. She says yes, but it turns out that Jon is able to take it to the laundry on the combi. She says it will be ready the next day. That day I text to see if it's ready. It's not. Tomorrow, she says. But it's not ready that day either. The following day, I tell her we'll come on the combi to get it, and she says to come after 4:00. Jon goes and gets it, and it has been washed, dried and folded perfectly but, now, we realize Ambar is unreliable.

Our neighbor, the person with the dogs that we share a courtyard with, has an outdoor washer which I've thought about asking if I could use, but she uses it a lot, to the point that I wonder if she takes in laundry. It seems rude to ask—particularly if she does take in laundry. I just feel like it would be weird for our neighbor to be doing our laundry. I ask her about the best place to take it, and she mentions a laundromat "a few blocks up the road," where they do it the same day, or you can do it yourself. We walk farther than a few blocks up the aforementioned road and find nothing. However, just a couple of blocks in another direction, just east of the plaza, in fact, (we live two blocks west of the plaza) we spy a place that looks like they do laundry and dry-cleaning. Actually, there's a dry cleaners right on our corner, but they don't take in washing.

Encouraged, we bring a sack of laundry to this place, where the very nice lady who runs it tells us, yes, we can leave it and have it back the next day after 7:00 p.m. because, she says, it gets sent off to a facility in Actopan, and that's when they return it.

We get it back on schedule and are pleased, except for the fact that there are a couple of items of clothing in the sack that don't belong to us. This is worrisome. If they've given us someone else's clothes, might not ours suffer the same fate? We bring the errant items back to the lady but she seems totally baffled about what to do with them.

Lo and behold, the next time we pick up our laundry from her, two things are missing. A pair of Jon's sweat pants that he really likes, and his Killers t-shirt! We ask her about it, but she is still baffled. She is as baffled about our missing items as she was about the extra items we returned. It is now our turn to be baffled. Yes, the laundry has been washed and dried, but it has moved on to the hell cycle. We write down a description of the items on a piece of paper, and ask her to check with the people at the facility in Actopan about it. She does, but to no avail. I do want to be clear; this is a lovely woman. We never have even a small moment of thinking she might be the one responsible for the loss of our clothes because, she, like all other shopkeepers we've encountered, is unfailingly honest. When she says she does not know where the clothing might be, we understand there is zero possibility that she is being anything less than truthful about it. She quite literally wouldn't know how.

There you have it; nobody knows anything about anything. She calmly explains with a smile, (as though we were Americanos), that since they just throw everyone's laundry in the same machines together, there's no guarantee you'll get back what you send. Oh, okay then… yes, I suppose that is an explanation of sorts. It's certainly not something we would have thought of in advance and since it's just the way of things, no one thought to mention it to us before us having the experience itself. Oh, and there's no reimbursement mentioned, nothing. Bafflement is our new state-of-being. What kind of a way is this to do laundry? Don't answer. We can replace the sweatpants, which weren't cheap, but the Killers t-shirt? Not likely. That, we decide, is the last time we're sending our laundry there.

However, she tells us she might have a solution for us! She calls up a local laundress friend of hers and tells her the situation. This, the lady says, is "unofficial," meaning she has to hide it from her boss, but she will send our laundry to the friend, who will do it for the same price, pick it up, and drop it back off. Perfect! When will it be ready? The next day, she says. But, the next day it's not there, nor the next, nor the next.

Who is this friend we ask? Her name is Ambar, the lady says. Oh my God! We're back to square one.

On our next laundry day, we pack our clothes into our small rolling suitcase, and schlep farther up the same road our neighbor had mentioned, almost all the way to the grocery store on the outskirts of town. We finally find the laundromat and, indeed, the lady there says she will do it, in its own separate washer, that same day, no problem. The trip there and back, twice in the same day, is worth about 15,000 steps alone, but it's the best solution we have so far.

At this point, Jon decides to order a mini washing machine from Amazon Mexico that will do a small load of clothes. We'll see.

This seems like a good time to talk more about our neighbor, Miriam. Miriam lives with her thirteen-year-old daughter, Maya, but we have seen no husband. I assume Miriam is divorced though I do spy a beefy looking guy who seems to drop by on occasion. I take to calling him her back door man. I finally introduce myself to him, but he seems unimpressed and barely grunts a greeting.

And then there are Miriam's dogs. For the first several days after we moved in, Chula, the fearsome Akita, would just bark and bark until late into the night, which would echo throughout our house and drive us absolutely bonkers. One night, around 10:00, I went to knock on Maya's window, which looks out into the courtyard, as Miriam didn't seem to be home, to ask if there was anything she could do to make Chula stop. She explained to me that Chula, who had been chained up since we moved in, didn't like it, and that's why she barked.

I said, "So let's unchain her?" I was really taken by surprise. Chula knew us by now and we knew she wasn't going to be aggressive with us. In fact, we had been passing an occasional treat to each of the dogs. Maya took the chain off, and that was extremely helpful as the dog quieted down a lot. It turned out Miriam had been leaving her chained for our sakes, not realizing it was unnecessary. We and the dogs had come to a mutual understanding, but had neglected to inform the rest of the neighborhood.

In general, we are coming to like our house more and more as we continue to fix it up. One of our most recent additions to the décor is a piece of artwork that Jon and I did together. From the same people we bought the lightbulb baskets from, we also purchased a large palm mat. Jon had an idea to paint it and hang it on the wall.

We bought some paints from the cute little craft shop in the plaza and Jon, using a flyswatter as a compass, created these cool geometric designs: a large circle in the middle, with triangles of color radiating to the edges in yellows, reds, greens, and purples. I painted little black hieroglyphic figures here and there—sort of like the ancient and the modern mixed together. Jon calls it "The Time Machine." We mounted it on the wall behind the couch and it really brings the living room together. We've also bought wooden chairs and a side-table, built by our now regular carpenter, to fill out the living room, and I made pillows by hand for the chairs and for the couch. We bought a coat rack made of 100-year-old wood for near the front door, and a *perchero*, a wall mounted rack for extra coats and bags, to go next to that. We've pretty much finished the painting and plastering, and added plants here and there to make it that much more homey.

One night, Marco comes by with his two young daughters and we sit around and chat. The daughters show us their artwork from school and sing mariachi songs. They are enchanting. Marco looks around the house with amazement. In the kitchen we've mounted little shelves that hold spices and things, and I've hung bunches of herbs from them. We've also bought these things called *despenseros*, kind of like stacked wooden display baskets, to hold food items and other things, and the effect is very charming. Inspired, Marco agrees to tile the horrible kitchen counter top, and to also tile the walls behind the sink and stove.

In the next few days he and Jon go choose the tile and, soon after, the tile guy, or *albañil* comes to do the job. It looks beautiful. This is really what the house needed to make it the Mexican home of our dreams. In spite of the non-existent water pressure, the lack of doors, the funky kitchen sink arrangement, and the fact that the occasional scorpion wanders in, we are coming to love it.

From Jon: About the scorpions: just before we moved in, Marco was very active in spraying insecticide all over the house, and was very proud to display that a few large scorpions had come out of their hiding places and were lying dead on the floor. I was appalled. Scorpions are not my favorite creatures. Of course, Lupita is an indoor cat, and we had to get Marco to install screens on the windows because that's not a thing in Mexico. He didn't exactly know what to do, or how screens across windows was a good thing, but he figured it out. After that, we would occasionally still see scorpions scuttling across the floor, and I quickly discovered what the chonck *in* chancla *meant (a* chancla *[chonk-la] is a flip-flop). I spent a lot of sleepless nights being concerned that Lupita would encounter one of these horrible nightmarish beasts and get stung, and who knows what that would do to a cat? Later, our neighbor informed us that cats love scorpions. They, being cats, mercilessly play with them until they die. This accounts for the fact that we often found random dead scorpions in the morning, thinking it was the spray still doing its job. No, it was the cat. How was I to know she was angry with me every time I killed a live one as it ambled across the floor? I was taking away a favorite toy. To be perfectly honest, I didn't just kill them. I fearlessly beat them at arms-length, into unrecognizable, squashed-oblivion with my handy* chancla. ¿Quién es más macho ahora? *Me! I'm the most macho!*

650,000 to 800,000 Steps

Last week I gave a presentation at the school for about 100 students and staff, in English, about Halloween. Since part of my job here is to teach about American culture, Rico has asked me to do four large-scale PowerPoint presentations this year: one for Halloween, one for Thanksgiving, one in the winter, maybe centered on Valentine's Day, and one in the spring, TBD.

I focused my presentation on the history of Halloween in Europe and the U.S., and on the New York City Greenwich Village Halloween parade, which I've attended more than once. The presentation was very well received, Rico was pleased, and I received a certificate. Why the certificate? I'm not sure.

Mexicans also celebrate a version of Halloween, though Day of the Dead is the major celebration this time of year. Today, the school is holding a Day of the Dead contest, and Rico has asked me to help judge. The contest consists of students who have dressed up in costumes representing *Catrinas* and *Catrines*, the traditional Day of the Dead icons, faces painted as skulls and wearing some version of Victorian/Mexican style clothes. This tradition is not exactly ancient but stems from the year 1910, when a man named José Guadalupe Posada drew a sketch for the newspaper depicting skeletons in fancy dress. The purpose was to satirize the Mexicans of the upper class, who were obsessed with rich Europeans, and tried to emulate them.

I'll also be judging the *ofrendas*, (offerings) which, in this case, are altars the size of small rooms, honoring a historical Mexican figure. They are decorated in flowers, especially the *cempasuchiles* (sem-pah-SOO-chee-les), the traditional orange flower of the holiday which resembles a large marigold. The altars are also decorated with photos of the deceased, crosses, *papel picado*, which are thin paper decorations cut in various designs, candles, sugar skulls, and food and drink that the deceased might have enjoyed. There is a lot of symbolism to these decorations, and pretty much everyone in Mexico creates their own altars using some variation of them to honor their own deceased relatives or ancestors.

Jon attends the event with me though he won't be judging. As we arrive, the students are still setting up their altars. We peruse them, impressed beyond words at how beautiful and intricate they are. I'm very excited about this event. It's going to be epic.

I am seated in the shade at a table with a green tablecloth, and the other judges come sit there as well. There are four of us in total. I have my bottle of water and I'm comfy there in the shade, pitying the students and others who have to endure the sun, and feeling very special.

First, there's some singing, as a kind of kick off to the event. Then, there's a beautiful dance performed by a troupe from the school to the song "Recuerdame" ("Remember Me") from the movie Coco. When, toward the end of the dance, they reveal photos of loved ones who have passed, I'm moved to tears. After that, Arlo and others perform in drag, boys dressed as girls and girls as boys, a traditional dance done to trick death, who dances among them, so that he doesn't recognize you if he comes to claim you.

Then, the parade of costumes begins. Jon is sitting in the shade with Rico nearby. We shoot each other astonished glances while each pair of *Catrinas* (the women) and *Catrines* (the men) come out to present themselves to the judges and the audience. One pair is what I call the "hipster *Catrines*," a beautiful girl with a long skirt made of shredded newspaper, and her partner in a stylish suit, their faces painted, as all the contestants' are, as skulls. Another girl has a skirt made of corn husks. Another is dressed as Sor Juana, a famous 17th century feminist nun. Another Catrina comes out on horseback, her partner leading the steed. Yet another pair are dressed as Aztec warriors. Each is so creative and stunning I find it impossible to rate them, but I must.

When this part of the festivity is finished, it's time to judge the altars. By the way, the contest was supposed to start at 10:00, but actually didn't commence until 11:00, so by this time it's about 1:00. I'm getting very hungry, and the sun has obliterated all shade. However, I go with the other judges to view the now finished altars, all of them in the blazing sun. I'm standing there with my green umbrella trying not to faint while the students read a long description of each of the altars, some in the hñähñu language. At this point, Jon ditches. He's had enough and I don't blame him. Off he goes, on the combi, back home. Even Rico has gone to seek the shelter of his office. The judging of the altars lasts about 45 minutes so now it's going on 2:00. I'm starving and dehydrated though I've already chugged the majority of my water. Finally, we judges are asked to make our decisions. We gather inside Docencia 2 and hash it out. I wish all the contestants could win, but I make concessions to the other judges because I need this to be over with. We hand our decisions in and, about 15 minutes later, the winners are announced and prizes handed out.

By now, I'm as dead as any of the ancestors. I stop by the cafeteria on my way out to get a bag of chips, a bottle of water, and a weird sandwich. I shove the chips into my mouth on my way to the combi, feeling genuinely faint.

Naturally, there's a line of students waiting to get on the combi. Mexicans are invariably polite except when it comes to waiting in line. They have no patience for that. The students are shoving their way onto the next combi as it arrives but I shove right back, and secure a coveted seat in the front by the driver. But, in getting on, I drop the bag of chips on the ground and the students are laughing about this which makes me furious. "*Respeto!*" I yell at them. Now,

I'm nearly in tears. The combi only takes about five minutes to get to the center of San Agustín, and I leap out, taking bites of my sandwich as I make my way home. When I get there, Jon is really worried about me because he knows how badly I handle too much heat and sun, not to mention going without food. My blood sugar is at rock bottom by this time, despite what I've managed to ingest, and while he fusses around trying to help me, I yell at him, crying, to leave me alone. All I need to do is eat! He makes himself scarce as I finish the weird sandwich and pass out on the couch. When I come to, I feel much better and apologize for my tantrum. He totally understands which is one reason he's the best husband in the world.

From Jon: Yes, it's true, I am.

Today, November 1st, is Jon's birthday, the date on which many Christian religions celebrate All Saints Day. In Mexico, that observance has merged with the Aztec belief that the souls of the dead existed in the afterworld and could return to the living, making it important to maintain a connection with those ancestors.

I don't think Jon has ever been that impressed that he shares his birthday with All Saints Day until now, in Mexico, where it's considered the best day of the year. Arlo wants to take us to the cemetery to show us how they honor the dead, and we want to go, but somehow it doesn't work out. We try to walk there, because we really want to see it decked out in all the traditional regalia, but we don't know exactly where it is, so we burn a lot of steps merely getting lost.

The town has come alive with preparations for honoring the dead. The *centro* is filled with flowers being sold for the occasion, like a giant garden in bloom. There are also stands set up with vendors selling all kinds of necessities for building an *ofrenda* or for decorating the cemetery: chocolate skulls, ghosts, nuns, and *Catrinas*; ceramic skulls, sugar skulls, *papel picado*; and of course *pan de muerto*. In general, the atmosphere is one of great celebration, with *micheladas*, beer with lime juice, sugar, and salt on the rim, sold everywhere. Jon calls them a waste of good beer.

Of course, Mexican people feel the loss of a loved one as deeply as anyone, but they find great comfort in knowing that the deceased come back to them once a year to visit and enjoy their favorite foods in the company of their family. Every artifact on the *ofrenda* has a meaning, most of which hail from the Aztecs, or Mexica (pronounced Meh-SHEE-cah), the true name of the ancient people of Mexico. The fragrance of the *cempasuchiles* helps guide the ancestors, as does a cross made of salt, representing the element of earth and intended as a path for them to follow. There is often a glass of water on the altar, as well as tequila, mezcal or beer, to quench their thirst and to represent the element of water. The strings of *papel picado* reminds us of how fragile life is, and represent the element of air, or wind. There are candles to light the way for the dead and to represent the element of fire. The sugar or chocolate skulls are sweets for the dead, as is the *pan de muerto*. And the photos, of course, are so we remember them in their physical incarnation. There is an enormous altar set up in the centro, honoring Francisco I. Madero, a former president of Mexico.

I've bought one of the ceramic skulls to bring back to the States with me for next year's Day of the Dead. I create a small altar on the dining room table with it for now, with some chocolate figurines and a candle. I bought a *cempasuchil* plant for the house, but I don't have any photos with me of deceased relatives. I would put tequila or beer out for my dad, but he stopped drinking decades before he died and I don't want to tempt him. I sure think of him today though, and all my grandparents who have passed, as well as dear friends of mine who died of AIDS many years ago.

This isn't a day to be sad though, as I've learned, and, anyway, we need to celebrate Jon's birthday, so of course we go to La Hacienda, where he has a deliciously prepared steak dinner and a huge slice of chocolate cake. Afterwards, as we're walking home, we notice that families with children are heading toward the plaza, all dressed in costumes, and so we join them. All of a sudden, we are accosted by three small children dressed as vampires. They grab Jon and hug him, yelling, "Happy Birthday!" I'm trying to figure out who they are until I notice Marco, grinning nearby. The children are his sweet little girls and their cousin. We give them some lollipops we've acquired along the way, and continue on to the *centro,* where children are trick-or-treating at all the stores, as per the American tradition, even though it's the 1st, and not the 31st. It is all a charming finale to Jon's birthday.

800,00 to 900,000 Steps

Today Arlo is determined to take us to the cemetery. Day of the Dead continues for three days so the festivities are hardly over with. He comes by at around 3:00 in his car, and we drive out in the direction where Jon and I had gone a few days before, but then veers off on a road behind the grocery store on the outskirts of town. We hadn't thought to go that way, figuring the cemetery would be visible from the main highway. It should be, because it's enormous, and has grown even more so with the addition of stands and stalls of venders selling food, alcohol, flowers, and sweets. The atmosphere, in fact, is one of a party. People are gathered around the stalls at tables and chairs, eating and drinking *loudly*. By this time in the afternoon, the alcohol has definitely started to take effect.

Arlo parks the car and we wander through this carnival to the entrance of the cemetery. There are throngs of people inside, and the *cempasuchiles*, candles, and food offerings are everywhere, on every grave and tomb. Jon and I figure that respectful solemnity is the correct attitude, but we're pretty much the only ones. Arlo leads us to his paternal grandmother's grave, covered with the orange flowers, and tells us what he knows of her, though he never met her. I don't know what became of his paternal grandfather, but his mother's parents are buried in her town, Tezontepec, about 45 minutes away.

We leave the grandmother's grave and meander through the maze of family tombs until we come upon a group of his friends. Arlo has friends *everywhere*. People all over town know him—after all, he grew up in San Agustín—yet no other local I've come to know is as popular as he is. If you're walking around town with Arlo, you can't make it five feet without someone stopping to greet him or vice versa. When I say stopping him to say hello, I do not mean a quick hello and goodbye. Each and every instance is a time to stop and have an animated conversation. People here love this guy and so do we.

The friends we've now stumbled upon are some combination of Arlo's cousins and pals, quite drunk on Micheladas, and they pull us right into their sphere. I don't really drink, and Jon is not inclined to sip from their offered cups, but their vibe is infectious, and we're laughing and talking up a storm in no time. In fact, this is the most fluid and relaxed my Spanish has been since we got here. I mean, I know my Spanish is excellent, but sometimes I get self-conscious and stumble. Having a few drinks is a great way to loosen up your language skills. Even though I'm not drinking, the inebriated mood is infectious.

After hanging out with this bunch for about a half an hour, we go back to Arlo's house where we're offered snacks from the large *ofrenda* set up in the carport of his house. Yes, people do eat the foods—sweets, nuts, and fruits, in particular—from the *ofrendas*. This is not my idea of dinner, so we head to the food court where Arlo shows us how he enjoys the *tacos dorados*, smothered in spicy *tomatillo* sauce with lettuce and cheese on top. We have been avoiding the lettuce in this food stand because we've been told to be especially careful of raw vegetables that possibly might not have been disinfected properly. We throw caution to the wind though, because we're celebrating with everyone else, and why not?

Two days later: we've made a horrible mistake.

The lettuce was clearly not disinfected and we're sick as dogs. To make matters worse, the pump that delivers water to our house has stopped working. We text Marco, and he reluctantly says he'll send a plumber over to inspect it, adding that the pump was working just fine when we moved in. Well, might I remind you that the house has been sitting empty and in disrepair for three years, so it's not surprising that the pump might not be in the best condition. We offer to pay for it, and the cost of the plumber, so we can get it fixed that day. I tell him I'll take it off the rent. Marco grumbles about this but I won't back down. We can't be without the toilets, especially not right now.

About an hour later, he comes by with the plumber and they tromp through the house, even though the cistern is in the patio, to double check that the problem isn't coming from the tank on the roof. In doing so, they leave one of the upstairs windows open with a ladder on one side and a chair on the other, an open invitation to a certain *gato* to feel free to explore.

When I discover the situation, I freak out because Lupita is nowhere in sight. So, as the plumber fixes the pump, Jon goes out onto Miriam's roof, which is attached to our house, to look for her. He spots her in the yard of the people who live next door, in a garden which has no access from our side.

I run around to the front of their house and bang on their door to let them know our cat is in their garden. No response. Miriam tells me she thinks they're out of town. Now, we're not only sick, with no working toilets, but we can't get to our cat, who may possibly disappear into the wilds of Mexico forever.

Finally, I have the idea for Jon to text the guy from the phone company, Topiltzin, whom Jon met when we were looking for houses that first week in San Agustín, because what we need is a ladder to get down into the garden.

Mercifully, Topiltzin responds, again, in the middle of his work day, and comes with a long ladder, which Jon uses to climb down from Miriam's roof to the other neighbor's garden. And yet, Lupita won't come to him. She runs off and hides and he can't get to her. She's having the time of her *pinche* Mexicana life (imagine any curse word you want for the translation of *pinche*). Topiltzin can't hang out all day, so he takes his ladder and goes, but not before Jon is able to prop up a rickety homemade ladder he's found lying in the yard.

He leans it against the wall and climbs up the good ladder, hoping that when the stupid cat decides she's finally going to come home, she can get out of the yard herself. We wait in suspense for about five hours, during which time the pump is fixed. Lo and behold, Lupita shows up outside the window precisely at dinner time and, with a small amount of coaxing, climbs back inside.

With usable toilets and our kitty home safe, we feel better. We eat some plain rice for dinner and call it a night.

900,000 to 1,010,000 Steps

I've met a lady at the university named Cristina who needs some English editing assistance. She's a Ph.D. in Chemistry who teaches there, and she's written a research paper that was rejected for publication because the English translation was poor. This is a good time to mention that the writing project I have been wanting to get going in San Agustín is going exactly nowhere. I've connected online with three women in other parts of Mexico by way of a contact I have in Mexico City, who are interested in working with me in kind of a mentorship situation meaning that they have their own writing projects which they'll share with me over time and I will help guide them to bring them to fruition in whatever way they choose. This way, I feel I have made some inroads in my project, but COMEXUS expects it to be a *community* project and those women are hardly in my immediate community.

I've made flyers and handed them out all over the place, announcing a live workshop, in Spanish, in which women can come together, to try their hand at any kind of writing: a diary, short stories, a memoir, essays, poetry, recipes...whatever suits them. My idea is that at each meeting they'll share the work they've done that week and we will talk about it, not to criticize, but to offer suggestions and encouragement. The flyer stresses, and I say it to everyone I talk to about it, that this is an opportunity to vent their feelings about life, family, work, or whatever they want. This is a chance to have a break from the day-to-day and to immerse themselves in something creative.

An impediment to this idea, however, is that women here in San Agustín work their fingers to the bone day and night. This is not an exaggeration. They run most of the shops and the stalls in the marketplace and food court, take care of their families, cook and clean, educate their children, and run side-businesses like selling baked goods or *mole* or whatever...in short, they do it all. I'm coming to understand that maybe this is why they don't have time for something as frivolous as a writing workshop. And yet, not only is my community project a requirement of my scholarship, but it's something I'm passionate about—the main reason, really, I applied for the Fulbright. I see this as a kind of research, continuing the track from my master's thesis which focused on female Mexican writers. I want to know what Mexican women would write about now, today—not published writers or famous writers—but everyday women, given the opportunity, or encouragement, to put their thoughts down on paper.

By the time I meet Cristina, it's the beginning of November. I'm desperate to get something started here in San Agustín and, frankly, grateful to have anything writing-related to work on with someone. In fact, I figure working on this paper is related to my community project because I'm helping someone in the community with their writing.

Cristina seems like a bit of a nervous woman. She's small—tiny really—and full of energy. She's upset about her spoken English, as well as what she has written. She feels it's not up to par. She tells me that ever since she had COVID, her brain hasn't been as sharp, and she can't remember words in either English or Spanish. We chat in both languages and, by the end of our meeting, I've agreed to take on her paper, which is a very scientific and technical text. I then tell her about my writing project. She assures me she will make it happen. She emphatically states that she will find the people and they will attend. I have no idea how she'll do this, but I'm grateful for the enthusiasm.

By now, we have mostly recovered from our stomach ailment. I'm determined to take Jon for a birthday trip to a nearby hot-spring. There's nothing Jon loves more than immersing himself in really hot water.

Arlo has assured us the hot-springs in his mom's home town of Tezontepec has a really nice "water park" as they call it, with naturally occurring hot-springs. The region we're in, the Valle del Mezquital, has hot-springs in abundance. People tell us the best one, the one we absolutely *have* to visit, is called Las Grutas de Tolantongo but it's a good two hours away and we're not up to that much travel at the moment. Tezontepec is just 45 minutes from San Agustín.

About 10:00 in the morning, we hop on a combi to Mixquiahuala (I know, I swore I'd never go to Mixquiahuala again but it's kind of a hub) and from there we get another one to Tezontepec. Once we clear Mixquiahuala, it's kind of a pretty drive. Tezontepec itself is an interesting looking town, but we don't have time to dawdle there. The combi driver tells us where to get off, and that the water park, El Huemac, is just down the road.

At this point, we could catch another combi to the park, but we decide we might as well walk, which we do, down a steep road, in the sun, that winds and winds for about twenty minutes until we reach the bottom, which is where a river runs through a lovely and fertile little agricultural valley. Once we arrive at El Huemac, we pay the admission and change into our bathing suits in a funky little bathroom for which they charge five pesos.

Pretty much every public bathroom in Mexico, unless it's in a museum, restaurant, or airport, charges five or six pesos. Sometimes you put your coins in a machine that opens the door for you, or sometimes there's an attendant you pay, who hands you a generous wad of toilet paper. This is all the toilet paper you're going to get, by the way, and though it's often more than you need, I've come to always carry tissues on me because you never know. Bathrooms simply don't come automatically equipped with toilet paper. Even in the bathrooms where there's no charge, you have to remember to get the toilet paper from a dispenser by the entrance because there won't be any in the stall. It's easy to forget to do if you're not used to it.

In this case, we pay the man the five pesos each, take the toilet paper and go into our respective bathrooms, which are, let's just say...adequate. In fact, El Huemac is basically just adequate overall. There's a big pool in the middle with kiddie slides and such, and beyond that a small outdoor pool, next to an indoor pool they refer to as the "spa." There's no place to put our stuff, but there's hardly anyone else here so we just set it down next to the pool and venture in. It's nice and clean, and the water is the perfect temperature for me though I know Jon likes it a little hotter. The spa is quite intriguing, a space with a low, curved ceiling that's very steamy, kind of like a *hammam*, one of those Turkish steam rooms, but with a pool. I like it in there, especially because it's out of the sun.

After lounging in the spa for a while, we head over to another, bigger pool, next to which is a spring from whence an enormous tree grows. The tree is actually in the pool and it's kind of amazing. The water is hotter there—a bit too hot for me. Anyway, we swim around for a while, mostly in the larger pool, then go to get some lunch, something that resembles quesadillas, from a lady grilling them up in a patio area where you can sit under umbrellas and eat. From this vantage point, the water park has a nice vibe, kind of like a Mexican seaside with cabanas. After that, we've done all there is to do, so we decide to head out.

The only problem is, we're not about to hike back up that hill and it is really hot by now. A guy at the entrance tells us that a combi stops there pretty often, and the occasional taxi goes by, so we wait it out in the blazing heat, huddled in whatever shade we can find, for about twenty minutes until the combi finally comes. Once it deposits us at the top of the hill in Tezontepec, we decide we've had enough of combis for the day and so we negotiate a trip back to San Agustín in one of the taxis that are hanging out near the combi stop.

This is not our first time in a Mexican taxi, but it is our first time in a taxi on the highway, and we are a bit disconcerted to find there are no seatbelts available. You just have to trust in God and say a prayer to the Virgen of Guadalupe that you will be delivered to your destination in one piece, which, thankfully, we are, for a price that would astound any foreigner: about four hundred pesos or twenty bucks for the 45-minute ride. Screw the bus and combi! Though perhaps we're taking our lives in our hands in a taxi, it's a much faster and more comfortable way to get around.

Another note about the taxis: the drivers in these rural areas of Mexico tend to be very friendly. This particular driver speaks a little English because he's spent some years in the U.S. He says he used to labor as a farm worker there, and relates how difficult and back-breaking the work is, and how dangerous. He lost his hair, he explains, because of the pesticides that are sprayed on the plants, chemicals that also harmed his lungs, which is why he had to quit and return to Mexico. He'd do it all again, he emphasizes, in a heartbeat, because the money is so good compared to what he can make doing pretty much anything in Mexico—definitely more than driving a taxi.

This makes me think about the hordes of people immigrating to the U.S. daily from Mexico and Central/South America, illegally or not. To me, Mexico is superior to the U.S. in terms of the strong and vibrant culture, and the way the people value their heritage and their families. And yet the conversation with the driver reminds me, if the poverty I see on a daily basis doesn't, that Americans live in a country with infinitely more possibilities and opportunities for people to improve their lives. We take it for granted every day, but people here in Mexico do not. Jon and I are far from rich, but we are quite wealthy compared to most people here. I'm humbled in the presence of this man who would give anything to return to a place that I value less and less because of the difficult politics, the rights I see being stripped away from women, and the justice denied people of color, and gay or trans people every day. At this point in history, Mexico is a more just place, politically. But I need to remember that the corruption and disorganization of the government has taken a huge toll on the economy over the decades, which affects everyone from the middle class down, and makes surviving day to day a genuine struggle. Needless to say, I tip the driver well.

1,010,000 to 1,100,000 Steps

The weather is turning cold at night. Even though, during the day, the temperatures get at least into the upper seventies and it's usually very sunny, the cold at night somehow penetrates the house much more so than the heat, leaving the downstairs chilly at all times of the day. The upstairs tends to be warmer, hot even, before the nights started cooling down so much, but no amount of heat seems to soak into the downstairs.

The weather in San Agustín, and in general throughout the Valle del Mezquital, is intensely dry, as the sun is intensely hot. If the sun is out, it burns. It's not like a nice, pleasant, basking in the warmth of a 75 degree day either; it's like: burning your face off unless you're in the shade. This is why I'm always going on about the sun and the heat.

The one thing I appreciate about this weather is that there is no, and I mean no, humidity. If it were humid, I don't think I could survive. We're going into the dry season now so it hardly rains. If it does happen to cloud over, it gets chilly right away because we're at such a high altitude. In other words, if the sun isn't shining, it's cool, but if it is, it's hot.

Related to that is the fact that I've lost approximately 5-7 pounds at this point, though I didn't have much to lose to start out with, and Jon has lost around 15. I appreciate losing a couple of pounds, but 5-7 is a lot for me and I am damn skinny at the moment. In fact, I've taken in many of my pants by hand since I can't find a tailor here to do it for me. And even though the weight loss is certainly due to all the steps, as well as the fact that we're eating so differently, I'm sure part of it is because the water has simply evaporated from our bodies.

I'm certain this is true because my skin has dried out and I feel a bit like a lizard these days. No amount of lotion, or even drinking a ton of water, seems to have a counter effect on the wrinkles I've acquired. So, what, I have to choose between being skinny or having smoother skin? Give me a moment... I'm thinking!

Anyway, because it's getting so chilly, Jon has ordered a couple of space heaters from Amazon to help with the situation. They don't do much to warm the house in general, but if you huddle in front of them, they help. We actually tried to find heaters in San Agustín, but we were told that people don't use them here because they *don't believe in them*. We were specifically told by a shop-keeper that the people of the area think artificially heated air is bad for one's health. She shared that piece of information with a totally straight-face. Jon and I had another of those moments of sharing a telepathic, *WHAT*? Who knows, maybe they're right, but I maintain freezing to death isn't all that good for your health either. This actually might be a possible explanation having to do with another puzzling phenomenon: we see many people all around town and in school wearing winter coats in 80 degree heat. This newly-revealed local aversion to heaters leads us to surmise that, since it's so cold in their homes they probably wear them inside, and keep them on outside just in case they might encounter a chill. Or, perhaps it's just the fashion. Neither of us has any intention of asking anyone about it. This particular mystery will just have to remain a mystery.

We embark on an extensive city-wide search for extra blankets. The wonderful people who run the shop where we found sheets don't sell blankets, but they told us to look for a black door across the street from the laundromat that lost our clothes, on the other side of the *centro*. (This is the accepted way of providing directions to anywhere so, by now, we're used to it, and know where to go. We're not savages anymore.) We actually find the black door but it's padlocked tight with a large chain. We're indecisively hovering around, wondering what to do, when a lady comes from around the corner, spies us, and motions us over. I have no idea how she knew what we were looking for but, it turns out, she has the keys to the door. We enter to find a kind of double shop, blankets neatly stacked on one side of it. We choose a couple of warm-looking ones, but it's the other half of the shop that really gets our attention. Displayed against one wall are several shelves of big pump-bottles filled with lotions and liquids, along with other interesting-looking items. A young woman appears, the lady's daughter, with a small baby in her arms. She charms us immediately with her bright smile. She speaks English and is eager to practice. She is the proprietor of this side of the double store. She makes and sells natural-products, telling us that she and her husband are the creators of all the lotions, soaps, shampoo bars, etc. Everything is made with biodegradable ingredients, and she can custom mix lotions to suit a clients' needs. A dream come true. I tell her how dry my skin is, and she concocts a mixture on-the-spot from a few of the lotions in the pump bottles, filling a smaller bottle for me to take. This, she says, I can come back with and refill, thus saving the plastic. In fact, you can bring any container and she'll fill it up for you. I buy the lotion, an oatmeal soap, and a shampoo bar made for dry hair, thrilled to have fallen into a place in San Agustín that not only sells natural products, but is so environmentally conscious overall. The young woman's name, we find out, is Anna. I don't know any other way to say it than it's like love at first sight between us. She's thrilled to have met us and immediately invites us to her family's *posada* in December (I will explain the *posada* later). Her mother, Naomi, now holding the baby, seconds this.

I also tell Anna about my writing workshop and she seems enthusiastic about it. Jon and I come away with our blankets and my products, feeling warmed already by meeting these delightful people. This, in fact, is the vibe we tend to get all over San Agustín.

Possibly it's all the sunshine but, though I try to avoid it at all costs, it seeps into your bloodstream. Jon and I walk around this town most of the time feeling almost high. This sense of euphoria is inexplicable though I suppose it could be the excess of Vitamin D. We love this place, we love these people, we even love the mangy dogs that are everywhere. They, like the people, are as friendly as anything.

From the first week we arrived here, we started to identify which shopkeepers were the friendliest, and who seemed to respond to our presence in a positive way. Most people, really, greet us with big smiles and a warm spirit, like Anna. Some don't and that is, I believe, either their nature, or they don't trust or like Americans, and who can blame them? Besides "annexing" a large part of their country, we've been like the bully next door, basically treating them like crap at every opportunity. As a result, I consider it kind of a miracle that many people in San Agustín not only accept us, but welcome us with open arms.

One of the shopkeepers who made us feel at home right away is a lady who we first referred to as the nut-lady (which had nothing to do with her level of sanity), until I learned her name was Rosalba. She doesn't so much run a shop as a stand in the marketplace, selling nuts, grains, oils, and all kinds of useful things. One day we fell into a conversation as she wanted to know what brought Jon and me to San Agustín. I explained about my scholarship and teaching at UPFIM, and I also mentioned the writing workshop to her, as I do to practically everyone I meet. She seemed genuinely interested in what I had to say, though not so much in the workshop. At any rate, she always greets us with "¿*Cómo estamos*?" "how are we?" and sends us on our way with blessings and good wishes. We're usually at her stand a couple of times a week and, yes, we give her lots of business, but I also think she genuinely likes us. We certainly like her.

Another of our favorites is Becki, who has a stand next to Rosalba's. Becki and her husband run a meat-market, which is also really just a stand in the marketplace. There are lots of meat-markets in store-fronts in San Agustín, some nicer than others, but we always end up at Becki's because, not only is she nice, but her meat is incredibly fresh and lean, and of the best quality. She grinds the beef or pork on demand, or will slice up some delicately thin pork cutlets, *chuletas,* for you. It's funny, you can't get chicken from a meat market, or *carnicería.* The chicken comes from a *pollería* and you better get it early in the day because, after around 3:00, we've discovered, they're sold out.

One of the first places we sniffed out in San Agustín (actually, it was Jon who found it), was a natural food market run by Lucinda. It was kind of a revelation to discover this shop because this was the only place where agave nectar could be found, which is a must-have in our diet, certain food supplements (including cayenne pepper), and gluten-free snacks. To be honest, we've given up on a gluten-free diet, which was something we mostly adhered to in Portland, because gluten-free products in Mexico, like bread or pasta, aren't very tasty and are extra hard to find. We received many blank looks when we dared to breech the subject of gluten-free anything. When we want snacks, we'll often go for the bad ones: potato chips, *chicharrones* (fried pork rinds or the non-meat version, which, frankly, is better), Cheetos (they're different in Mexico), Doritos... What difference does it make? We still continue to lose weight. Not only that, but my cystitis is pretty much cured. I don't know what exactly made the difference, but I can now eat spicy foods, citrus, tomatoes—whatever I want with little to no ill effects. I call it the Miracle of Mexico. Could it be the water? Not unless it's the filtered kind we get delivered every week.

But I digress. Lucinda is as kind as can be and we quickly become regulars. We've also become fond of a sweet young woman with a lovely smile who sells eggs out of the back of her car, which sits in front of her shoe store. Also, there's a guy who squeezes oranges for fresh juice from the back of his pickup truck. He's the one who taught Jon his first words in hñähñu: *haxajuä,* (pronounced *ah-sha-waaaaaaah),* meaning "good morning." And let's not forget the kind and very ancient lady who runs what people here call "the big store," a not really very big store that sells housewares. We have received more blessings from her than anyone because she never lets us leave without telling us how much we are loved and protected by God, Jesus, and/or the Virgin Mary. Jon suspects there are also several ancient native deities whom she has entrusted with our care.

Another of the amazing women I've met here is Isabel. She owns a popular hair salon called Linda Mujer. Once we'd been here a couple of months, I needed a haircut. I've been going to a curly hair specialist in Portland, and before that in New York for the past 15 years or so. I am very picky about the way my hair is cut. However, since Isabel's salon is right around the corner from where we live, and there aren't a ton of other choices, I decided I may as well check it out. When I went in and talked to her about cutting my hair, she told me that she wasn't familiar with cutting curly hair, as most Mexican women have straight hair. Still, we agreed that I would explain the technique, and she'd give it a try. I have to say, she didn't do a bad job. Inspired, due to having run out of the hair dye I brought with me, I decided I'd trust her with coloring my hair as well. Try as I might, in all the stores that sell it, and many do, I could not find a color to equal mine. People don't tend to dye their hair red here. Though I'm a natural redhead, I still want to cover the grey.

I made another appointment, and she and I carefully perused the color options. We agreed on one that was kind of a coppery red—maybe not the color I was used to—but I realized I'd have to try something different if I didn't want my hair to completely fade. Let's just say, it did not turn out quite like I had, perhaps wishfully, expected. It was bright! It was really, really, really bright and, honestly, I don't need something else that makes me stand out more than I do here. Still, what choice did I have? I had to live with it and still do. In fact, I'm typing this in the glow of my hair. On the upside, her services are incredibly reasonable. She also gave me a gel manicure for the equivalent of about five American dollars. Beyond that, I really enjoy chatting with her. She's been through a lot, including the death of her husband to COVID two years ago, which she opened up to me about with great sadness. Yet, in spite of the challenges she faces, she maintains a great sense of humor and is incredibly strong.

I'm inspired by all the women I meet here. If only I could get them to write something down, anything, really, to share with me, whether they actually attend my (non-existent) workshop or not. Yet, like I said, no one has the time. What did I expect?

1,100,000 to 1,190,000 Steps

Thanksgiving is nearly upon us. Jon and I had planned a Thanksgiving party at our house for the Sunday after since no one has the day off on Thursday. We'd planned to make cornbread stuffing with chorizo and dried cranberries, roasted *calabacitas*—a kind of round zucchini and the only kind of squash we can find around here; pick up a couple of the roasted chickens from the food court since I haven't seen any turkeys available (though they're native to Mexico), plus some tortillas from our favorite *tortillería*, and an apple crisp for dessert.

I've done my presentation on Thanksgiving for the school, focusing on two things: the National Day of Mourning, which is Thanksgiving from the Native American perspective, and how my family acknowledges the genocide of a people, while we also gather with our loved ones to give thanks for what we have. (I received another certificate for this presentation, and they also gave me one for judging the Day of the Dead contest. I'm starting a collection.)

However, the day after my presentation, which was the day before official Thanksgiving, Jon and I fell ill, again, with some horrible stomach ailment. What did we eat this time? I have no idea. I texted the invitees to tell them we have to postpone for the following Saturday, which is the day after my birthday.

My birthday has arrived and with it good health. I'm taking the day off from school, but yesterday Rico surprised me with a little party, only attended by Lina, Alberto, me, him, and a staff lady at the school whom I've come to know because she comes to my English chat sessions. I walked into the office about 3:00 p.m., not expecting it at all, and when I saw the cake and people gathered, figured it was for something else. But then Alberto, ever the teaser, said, "Are we going to eat your birthday cake without you?" and I realized the party was for me. Now, as you know, I try not to eat refined sugar. I have issues with my blood sugar and what white sugar does to it. Especially, if I eat sugar during the day, it can really send me into a spin. But, what was I going to do? I could pull my usual 'oh, I'll take a piece home and eat it later,' but that seemed rude, so I asked Lina to cut me a small slice. It was a cheesecake that Rico had bought in Pachuca—absolutely delicious. Then they sang me *Las Mañanitas*, which is the Mexican birthday song, in several verses. It's a little hard to understand the lyrics, but it sounds very sweet.

I hung out and chatted with everyone for a while, waiting for the blood sugar crash, but it never came. This is a revelation! I'm starting to clue into the reality that, in this region, they sweeten most desserts with *piloncillo*, which is dried sugar cane juice, brown and unrefined. It seems as though I can eat it, within reason, without a problem. The lightbulb is flickering on over my head. It's very likely that's what this cake was sweetened with. Jon and I actually had several, somewhat embarrassing, encounters in various stores asking if they carried organic or unprocessed sugar. The looks we received translated to, "What are these *locacillos* (little crazy ones) wanting now?" All this time we'd been searching for the very thing that was right in front of us. *Piloncillo* is sold in virtually every store and throughout the marketplace. It looks like little conical brown cakes. It is so inexpensive that when Jon wanted to buy three of them to see how to use them, the seller insisted that he take five more, because he did not have change for a single peso. White sugar is very rarely seen here because it's so expensive.

Anyway, we divvied the cake up, and I took home about a quarter of it for me and Jon to nibble on over the next few days.

Getting back to today: I decided I want to go somewhere different, besides La Hacienda, though there really is little else in

San Agustín. Oh, I forgot to mention that a Japanese restaurant recently opened up just a block from us. I think it was Miriam who first told us about it though one day we ran into Anna and her husband, who had just come from having dinner there. We tried it and it wasn't bad! It also wasn't exactly Japanese, but there was a close resemblance, and was a welcome something new to add to our diet.

Yet, even though it's a tradition for me to have sushi on my birthday, the Japanese place isn't upscale enough for what I have in mind. Instead, I tell Jon I want to go to Actopan to see the 17th century convent that the town is famous for, and to find a nice place to eat. I think it's time we give Actopan a chance.

We head out on the bus at about 4:00. Half an hour later we arrive in the main intersection of Actopan where all the buses stop. We ask which way to the *centro,* and a nice lady not only points us in the right direction, but actually walks us there.

We follow her along the pleasantly bustling street, filled with shops, eateries, and bakeries, about five blocks in all, until we get to the town center, and bid our guide *adiós*. The *centro* is absolutely lovely—green and grassy with a pretty gazebo in the middle, and very clean. On one side of the square is the Hotel Convento, built in the colonial style. In fact, all the buildings around the center are in that style, which, of course, is typical. But on the opposite side of the square flanked by shops, is the cobblestone alleyway that leads to the convent with some interesting looking restaurants along the way.

The former Convento de San Nicolás de Tolentino is at the end of the alleyway, across a large plaza. We are astounded by its beauty and size. Built of grey stone, it soars into the air, walls topped with turrets, and on one side of the building is a bell tower that rises even higher. The massive main door to the sanctuary looks like it's made of the original, four-hundred-year-old wood.

The sanctuary is about to close, but we're able to go in and look around. The stone work of the ceiling is impressive, as are the original murals in muted tones. Back outside, we head around the corner of the main building to check out the giant open-air chapel which, according to the information on a sign, was built to get the native people to attend mass since they didn't like being enclosed in a building. There are murals inside the half-dome of the chapel telling stories of Christ's life so that the people could understand without knowing how to read. Very clever of those Spaniards.

From Jon: Devious is a better word.

Beyond this, there's not much to see. The gardens closed at 3:00, which we didn't know, and the stalls that made up a nearby marketplace are now closing. It's still a bit early for dinner, but (as usual) we're hungry, so we wander back to one of the restaurants along the way.

Lina had told me of a place that serves local and native foods that she highly recommended but a restaurant with a rooftop garden catches our eye. Ladies are making fresh tortillas just inside and that's always a good sign. Realistically, it's not like any restaurant would dare to serve anything but fresh tortillas here. The locals would not go for that. They might even become incensed enough to bring out the torches and pitchforks. Pre-made tortillas? Please!

A host ushers us up the stairs, where we find a lush space overlooking the plaza and the convent. We have a delicious dinner, but now I'm curious about the place with the native food. This simply means we'll have to come back to Actopan another time. It has turned out to be a pretty inviting place, and I now see what Lina sees in it, but I'm still glad we didn't end up living here. It is, indeed, a nice town, certainly with more amenities than San Agustín. And yet, it doesn't have what I consider to be San Agustín's charm, which I think comes from a small community where everyone knows each other, and where everyone rallies together to make life better for all.

Today is the day of our Thanksgiving party, a week late, but it's the thought that counts. We've invited around fourteen people, which means some will have to eat at the coffee table in the living room, but I'm pretty sure not everyone will show up. In fact, Rico has already sent his regrets, as he and his family would have to come from as far as Pachuca, and he has other obligations. Anna is busy with the baby, as she often is, so they can't come either.

We've scheduled the party to begin at 4:00, figuring it's sometime between the main meal and suppertime. 4:30 rolls around and no one has arrived. At 5:00, Arlo appears, but without his boyfriend, who's not in town. Thank God we at least have one attendee. By the way, when I invited our neighbors, I committed another lovely little faux pas by asking Miriam if she and Maya would like to attend. Miriam wrote me back asking if she could bring her husband. So, the guy I've been calling her back-door man is actually her husband. She's not a single mom like I thought, and she probably thought it was rude of me to invite her and her daughter, but not her husband. Maybe she thinks, in spite of Jon, I hate men, or just don't like her husband, though I've only seen him on those couple of occasions and don't even know his name.

Just as I'm starting to worry that Arlo will be our only guest, Miriam, her husband *Claudio*, and Maya show up. Now things are starting to roll. Then, about a half an hour later, Marco and his dad, Fernando, arrive. I ask why they haven't brought Maria, and Marco's daughters, but it turns out the little ones are sick and their grandmother has stayed home to take care of them.

Now, we have a solid dinner party with six guests, a total of eight altogether, including us, and everyone dives into the food, especially impressed with the stuffing. The menu is the same as what I'd originally planned: the cornbread/chorizo stuffing with cranberries, two roasted chickens from the food court, roasted *calabacitas*, mashed potatoes, tortillas (because they're a must with every meal) and apple crumble for dessert. No gravy, sorry. I just couldn't figure out how to make it with no bird roasting in the oven.

I was worried about the stuffing because it's a food they're not the least bit familiar with, but everyone loves it, especially Arlo who has helping after helping.

We eat and chat convivially for a couple of hours, both in English and Spanish, though some of the guests only speak Spanish, and Jon only English. He understands Spanish pretty well, however, and manages to keep up. Somehow, we get into a conversation about the National Day of Mourning, and Fernando asks me to explain it along with the history of Thanksgiving, which I do. This leads to all kinds of other deep topics, just the kind of conversation I love.

Maya is quite a shy young woman, and barely speaks, but seems to listen to it all with interest. At some point, she leaves, and comes back with a kitten they've recently acquired. Along with their two dogs, they also have five cats that mostly stay inside. The kitten provides an icebreaker between us and Maya, and we realize that, in spite of her silence, she likes us, and likes having us as neighbors. This is the moment we really connect with Miriam and Maya, and Claudio too. He's a large man, like his cousin Marco, a bit gruff, but has a great sense of humor and a generous spirit. It's interesting that Marco and Claudio get along famously, since it's been made clear that the two sides of the family have issues with one another. This has something to do with their mothers, sisters who at some point had a falling out, and have remained at odds ever since. The boys, on the other hand, are still just boys with one another, vying with each other to see who can endure the hottest hot-sauce on their food. Jon takes this opportunity to introduce them to cayenne (strangely, this pepper is not well known here). They both apply it with gusto and while they say nothing outwardly, both their faces go red and they dab at their foreheads with napkins. Jon's stature as El Patron rises.

When the party wraps up, I offer leftovers for the taking, and Arlo enthusiastically accepts a portion of stuffing and the apple crisp

I served for dessert. Even so, we have so much stuffing leftover, I put it in the freezer for Christmas.

1,190,000 to 1,260,000 Steps

Now that we're into the first week of December, classes have essentially evaporated, which they actually started to do not long after Day of the Dead. November is a time when the teachers give their evaluations and the quarter is winding down. Often, when the teachers give evaluations, they tell me not to bother coming to class because they don't need me to help with those, except for the oral exams. I continue to run my English workshops and chat sessions throughout November, but I can't really get anyone to show up during these early days of December. I'm still fretting about my writing workshop, even though Cristina continues to say she'll make it happen. She and I have been getting close, which is really nice, and have had a couple of lunches together in restaurants not far from the school (which, of course, close by around 5:00 pm). In fact, she's dying to take Jon and I on an excursion, and texted me the day after my birthday, wanting to take us to Actopan. I regretted to tell her we went by ourselves the day before. Undeterred, she said she wants to take us to the archeological site near the town of Tula, about forty-five minutes away, and today is that day.

We have a little trouble meeting up, because it's a Sunday, *tianguis* day, and she can't get through the town to our house, so we agree to meet by the combi stop, but she can't find that either, so by the time we do connect (she lives in Actopan and isn't that familiar with San Agustín), we're about a half an hour late getting started. That's okay, it's still only 10:30 in the morning. In the car with Cristina is her daughter, Marina, an incredibly bright young woman of nineteen, who speaks nearly perfect English. On the way, we meet a woman from the school, Estela, and her two daughters, in their own car, and they caravan with us to Tula.

As we drive, Cristina tells me the best news possible. She and Estela have got a group of women from the school who are interested in my workshop and want to start that very week. She says they are a combination of some staff members, like her and Estela, and graduate students in her Chemistry department.

The timing seems a little awkward for starting a new endeavor, since school is about to break for Christmas. Plus, there's the fact that I have to leave in early January for the mid-term reunion of the ETAs in La Paz, Baja California Sur which means, once we do break for Christmas, I won't see the group again until mid-January. Still, I agree that it makes sense to start now and get a little momentum going. The women can be working on their writing projects during the interim, I figure, so they'll have something to present after the break, and we can at least have two meetings before then.

I am soaring with joy and excitement. Finally, finally, my workshop is coming together. Just so you know, I haven't been doing nothing in terms of my community project while waiting for this to happen. Since Anna turned out to not really have an interest in writing, I suggested to her that we start an English conversation group, and she offered to host it in her shop, which we figured would be a win/win because the people who attended would maybe buy her products too. She was so enthusiastic that she said she'd spread the word throughout town, and make a sign for the shop door. I made up a flyer which I gave to her and also disseminated everywhere I could.

And yet, no one but Anna, her sister, her mom, and the baby ever showed up. I didn't mind because I loved chatting with them. I was thrilled to help Anna with her English, even though her mom and sister didn't speak the language at all. Anna and I translated for them and it was a congenial gathering. The conversation group never expanded beyond Anna's family, and it hasn't taken place every week either because sometimes the baby is sick or they have other plans. I'm starting to learn that's just how things are in San Agustín. People are busy and have to take care of the business of day-to-day life, often in order just to survive. Just because some random redhead shows up in town to tell them they should learn to express themselves through writing, or to speak English, doesn't mean they will.

Today, though, I realize that my purpose here in San Agustín, besides, of course, my classes at the uni seems to be coming to fruition. Not only that but Jon and I are about to have an illuminating experience in Tula because Cristina, though a chemist by trade, is also an expert in Mexican history, especially of the Valle del Mezquital.

We arrive at the archeological site and Jon and I pay the entrance, which is free to Mexican citizens on Sundays. Though probably not necessary, Cristina engages one of the guides who offers their services near the entrance of the park for merely the price of a tip afterwards. This lady explains the flora on display as we walk the half-mile or so through desert vegetation and three corridors of *tchotchkes*, but I only listen with half an ear because a) I don't like tours, and b) I grew up in the southwestern desert of the U.S. and the landscape and plant life is very similar to this region. Jon isn't paying any attention, partly because the tour is being conducted in Spanish, but also because he's deep in conversation with Marina, who is a rock and mineral fanatic, and a big science fiction reader like he is; in other words, they're both nerds. So the lady is mostly targeting her speech to Estela and her group because Cristina is explaining extra bits of information to me on the side and I find her much more interesting.

When we arrive at the site of the ruins, we stop in our tracks, awe struck. Rising before us is a pyramid, on top of which is a platform with eight or so enormous stone pillars, carved to represent Toltec warriors. I've seen photos of these figures, generally referred to simply as The Toltecs, or Los Atlantes, but seeing them in person is unbelievably impressive. If you are ever in Mexico City, or anywhere else in the vicinity, make this a day trip. You'll be glad you did.

And yet, the pyramid is only one aspect of this ancient city, built for the emperors and priests from whence to rule over the populace, which, in its day, was spread over the valley. Now, you can see the modern city of Tula just to the east but, apparently, the buildings were built on top of the ancient town. In other words, if one could excavate beneath the homes and buildings that are there now, one would find many more of the ruins of this once great civilization.

Before we go to explore the pyramid, we hike around a nearby structure that was once a game field. The game that was played here was kind of like soccer, I understand, but the loser also lost his head. Yes, the Toltecs were a violent people, but they were basically taking their cues from the Mexica of Teotihuacan, from whence they fled somewhere between 300-600 A.D. when that civilization, just northeast of Mexico City, began to fall. Hey look, don't quote me on this stuff. I'm not pretending to be an expert. I'm just passing along the information I take in, and it seems to be a little hazy in general because even the experts have been left to conjecture, somewhat, about these ancient civilizations and what took place back then.

After perusing the game field, we head over to the pyramid and observe some intricate carvings on the walls of the surrounding structures. Cristina informs me these used to be painted in vivid colors, and bedecked with turquoise, jade, sapphire and other semi-precious stones. It's hard to imagine the full splendor of the ancient city, and yet splendid is exactly what it was. On the other side of the pyramid are a series of *Chac Mools* without their heads. A *Chac Mool* (pronounced chahk-mohl) is a ceremonial figure in a reclining position, belly up, with a squarish head and large ears. These were a sort of bench on which people were beheaded and their blood collected. However, these *Chac Mools* are also beheaded because their noggins were removed and carried off as trophies by later civilizations who raided the area.

Finally, we climb the pyramid, not easy to do because the steps are very narrow and steep. But we all accomplish it, and then are able to stand amongst the warrior statues and marvel at the solemn immensity of them. From here, we can see some of the distant volcanoes, considered sacred to the Toltecs, as well as the entire valley of and around Tula. At this point, Cristina shares with us the fun fact about how the priests would use the heads of their enemies, and I think also the losers of the ball game, as bowls from whence to eat their version of *posole*, a favorite Mexican soup. Mmmm, yum.

The guide wraps up her tour at this point and we tip her, but we're not done with our excursion because, back on the ground, there's more to see: another pyramid, that of the sun, which we're not allowed to climb, another playing field, and a long, low stone structure which was the site of more human sacrifices. After roaming around the area for a while, we head back along the half-mile path, through the corridors of *tchotchkes* (where Jon buys a t-shirt) and to the car.

Now, we're off to have lunch in Tula. Cristina takes the group to a modern looking restaurant that's kind of like a diner. The menu looks great, and I order the enchiladas with *salsa verde*, which is quickly becoming one of my favorite dishes in Mexico. Cristina practically insists I have the steak, which is what she's having, but I'm dying for those enchiladas. I'm glad I didn't cave because they are delicious and I inhale them. At this point we strike up a conversation in which the word "prickly" comes up. We're speaking English with Cristina and Marina so that Jon can join in, and Estela's daughters understand it too, though Estela not so much. Jon explains the word prickly to Marina, who picks it up right away and decides it describes her mother well. I haven't really seen this side of Cristina, though I might describe her as high strung and a bit controlling.

When no one's paying attention, I whisper to Jon that we should pick up the tab to thank everyone for taking us on this wonderful excursion. He, of course, agrees, so I excuse myself to use the restroom and, on the way back, stop our waitress and ask her to make sure to give us the bill. She takes my credit card then and there to avoid any awkwardness. A few minutes later, she comes to see if anyone wants dessert or coffee and, once that's established, Cristina asks for the check. The waitress tells her it's been taken care of. The look that comes over Cristina's face is almost frightening. She is incredulous. How can this be, she demands. I tell her we took care of it.

Her face reddens with anger. "What? No!" She seems to not be able to take in this information. "No! I pay! I invited you!"

"No, no," I say gently, surprised at her reaction. I explain we wanted to thank her for bringing us to the archeological site and being such a wonderful guide.

I can see she is completely irate, though trying hard not to raise her voice or lose her temper as she protests.

"It's too late," I say, trying to placate her. "Don't worry about it. It was our pleasure."

Now, she sort of sputteringly explains to us that, when a Mexican invites you to a meal, they pay. Period. No ifs, ands, or buts. Not to allow them to is incredibly rude.

It's now my turn to be astonished. I figured it was like it is in the U.S. If someone offers to pay, but someone else gets to the check first, you might argue about it but nobody gets offended, and someone eventually gives in.

Marina and the others seem more amused by this exchange than anything else, but Marina does confirm what her mother said. I apologize profusely, and repeat that I just wanted to thank them for the trip today and all their attention. Anyway, there's nothing anyone can do because the bill has been paid.

In the car afterwards, we're finally able to joke about it. Cristina kids that the reason Mexicans want to know ahead of time if you're picking up the check is so that they can order as much as they want. We all laugh, but I feel I've learned a valuable cultural lesson from my faux pas. If you want to pay for a meal in Mexico, you must say ahead of time that you are inviting the others. That settles it once and for all.

1,260,000 to 1,320,000 Steps

Today is the day of my first writing workshop and I dread that nobody will show up. The room has been chosen, I've prepared activities, and I'm excited and nervous.

Cristina and Estela meet me at the appointed room, with a couple of their female master's students in tow. Hmmm, four people. That's not what I was expecting. Cristina said there would be eleven. Yet, over the course of the next fifteen minutes or so, more show up—all eleven, in fact.

Now, I'm genuinely excited. I explain the idea of the workshop, and we talk about what kinds of projects they might select. I get the feeling the master's students are really there because they want help with their thesis papers in English. This is not exactly the purpose of the workshop, but I'm sort of desperate to hold their interest so I suggest that academic writing can definitely be a project choice. Even though the purpose of the workshop is not for me to correct and edit their English, I would be willing to help them out with their papers.

These women are strong and smart. Someone brings up that some of their male counterparts have taken an interest in the workshop too, and can they be included? I explain that the reason I want this workshop to be for women is so that they can have a safe space to express themselves without the censure, self or otherwise, that the presence of men can create.

Cristina argues it is a more feminist position to have men present if they want to be, to hear what women have to say about their bodies, children, childbirth, violation, subjugation, etc. She says men need to hear it and we shouldn't be afraid, like many of our mothers were, to talk about female issues and concerns in front of males.

In other words, time for men to man up about it

She's convinced me. I love this point of view. We agree men can be included.

Next, I give them some time to write an informal proposal of their project and then share with the group. Cristina has the idea to write a cookbook with native recipes of the hñähñu people who are her ancestors, using local ingredients from the Mezquital Valley, in the three languages, hñähñu, Spanish, and English, with me doing the translation. Another young woman will write a memoire for her young daughter of her life so far. Others have ideas about short stories, and of course their academic papers.

Then we talk about what we should name the group, and someone comes up with: Caution, Women Writing (even though it may include men, they can just suck it up). I collect their contact numbers so I can create a WhatsApp group and we're off and running. The workshop concludes after an hour, we agree to meet at the same time and place the following week, which will be our last meeting before the break. I leave there walking on air. This is exactly what I wanted from my community project. I have Cristina to thank for this. She is a marvel.

Sunday rolls around, which, of course, is *tianguis* day. Jon and I feel like the house is ready for our Christmas visitors in just another two weeks, so we don't need to buy much besides some weekly supplies, and start stocking up on Christmas decorations. We've been wondering what to do about a Christmas tree, because I...

Tjjjjkkklsahhhh (Sorry, Lupita just walked across the computer.)

...don't like fake trees and that's all they have here. It's no wonder. They don't grow Christmas trees, and importing them would cost a fortune. I'm used to living in Oregon where trees basically grow on trees. As we wander around, we see that "the plant lady" has potted evergreens for sale. They are only about three feet tall, and aren't really of the Christmas tree variety, but they would do. So, for about

80 pesos (four dollars) we buy one and put it in a place of honor in the living room. It's beginning to feel a bit like Christmas.

Every *tianguis* day we meander up the street where La Hacienda is located, to see what the second-hand vendors have for sale. This street is also where one of our carpenters has his stuff for sale on one corner, as well as the basket guy on the opposite corner. Recently, we purchased a "matrimonial" or full sized bed platform—the kind with drawers underneath, from the carpenter, to put in our guest room with the mattress the Peace Corps girl left behind. This will be mom's room when the family comes for Christmas, and for other friends whom I'm anticipating will visit. We've also bought a gel foam topper for it because the mattress is hard, as in *hard*, and some nice warm blankets now that we know where to get them.

Anyway, it's on this street that I often stop at one of the vendors' stalls where I've found used tops and sweaters I liked. The person that runs it, along with her husband, is a tiny young woman whom I strike up a conversation with every time I'm there. I call her tiny because she's about 4'10", but she's almost as round as she is tall. Her name is Gabriela and she has a great sense of humor. We always joke together, though she uses slang and expressions that are sometimes hard for me to understand. She's told me that she and her husband are of the hñähñu tribe, though she doesn't really speak the language other than a few words. I'm fascinated by this. She, in turn, is fascinated with me, always referring to me as a doll, or a model. She thinks I'm gorgeous, especially obsessed with my blue eyes. At my age, I'll take all the admiration I can get. Yet, I've genuinely come to like her and her husband, Antonio. We've even exchanged numbers though it's taken us a few tries to connect. Now that we're in touch on WhatsApp, she's really wanting to invite us over for dinner, to her house, which is somewhere outside of San Agustín. I'm reluctant to take her up on it partly because I know they are very poor and I'm not sure I'm ready to have a meal at her house if it's like some of the run-down shacks I've seen here and there, in and around San Agustín. Mixed in with some veritable mansions, and sometimes side-by-side, there are some real hovels in this town. I'm not trying to be a snob; I just worry that it won't be clean or...I don't know. I don't know what I imagine, but I'm not sure I'm up for the reality of it. And so, I put her off, letting her know I'm preparing for my family to come visit at Christmastime, and suggesting that, when we do get together, maybe we should do it at my house. She's clearly very proud of her home and her cooking though, so we'll see.

Today is the day of the second meeting of Caution, Women Writing. I go to the room at the appointed time, but only one person is there. We can't figure out where everyone else is. Did they change the room? This is a fairly common occurrence at UPFIM. I can't communicate with anyone via WhatsApp from my location, Docencia 2, because I have no service here. Rico always acts a little surprised that I have so much trouble connecting to the school wi-fi when I'm not in the office, but nobody has told me what I need to do to get school-wide access though I've asked many people. Oh well.

The student gets through and Cristina tells her they've had to cancel. Damn it! I had a feeling something like this was going to happen! I'm trying to be patient; I'm trying to be understanding, but I just don't get it. How could we have had such a great meeting last week and, now, everyone has baled! I'm beyond frustrated.

Cristina texts me later and asks me to meet her for lunch at our favorite haunt tomorrow and she'll explain. Explain? I don't want explanations; I want a workshop!

Over lunch today, she tells me what happened. The school is having a shift in administration, and they fired most of the women who are in my workshop. This is hard for me to understand because those women are master's students. How do you fire a student? Well, they did, or they kicked them out, or something. Needless to say, yesterday, everyone was really upset and not inclined to go to the workshop, seeing as how they weren't going to be students in the school anymore, and the rest were upset for them, and they ended up meeting to discuss taking legal action against the school. What a mess! I guess even Arlo is in danger of losing his job, and Cristina isn't feeling secure about funding for her research.

    I leave after lunch feeling really defeated. Cristina told me not to worry, that we would regroup in January, but it's just one more setback. I swear I could cry.

1,320,000 to 1,400,000 Steps

To assuage my disappointment about the workshop, Jon and I decide to head to one of the Magical Towns in Hidalgo, Real del Monte. We've been trying to coordinate with Rico to go with him and his family, but either we've had to cancel for one reason or another, or he has. So, rather than rely on him, we decided today was the day to get out of San Agustín and take a little day trip.

We board the horrible bus and endure the hour and fifteen-minute ride to Pachuca, where we get off at the Central de Autobuses. There, we get a taxi to Real del Monte, just a fifteen-minute drive up into the mountains above Pachuca. The cab driver is playing classical music on the radio, and Beethoven serenades us as we leave the high desert landscape and enter a more Oregon-esque area of pines and greenery.

Here's something you should know about the Magical Towns of Mexico: this is an official designation given to towns that have something really special about them, which, based on my limited understanding, includes either architectural beauty, a unique history, archeological points of interest, some distinctive geographical feature, etc. Also, it must adhere to certain standards, for instance the smaller Magical Towns cannot have any overhead electrical wires—they must be buried. The town must also have certain safety standards and services for visitors. There are other criteria as well, but those are the ones that stand out for me. At the time of my writing this, Mexico has 177 Magical Towns.

Real del Monte is quite small, and very hilly, with cobbled streets, and mountain vistas all around. We are here on a sunny day though I understand it often is rainy and cloudy. It's also quite a bit cooler than in San Agustín, as is Pachuca, being so much higher. Real del Monte used to be a silver and gold mining town—this is one of the things that makes it special—the history. It was the Spanish who "discovered" the precious metals here, but Cornish miners came from England in the 1800s and developed the area. They also brought soccer with them, and a food known as pasties (in Spanish, it's spelled *pastes* and pronounced "pahs-tehs"). They have *pastes* in San Agustín, but this is where they originated, right here in Real del Monte, a flaky, handheld pie, stuffed with all varieties of fillings, which made the perfect, portable food for the miners. My mom makes a version of them, and many Americans are familiar with them, especially if they're of British origin. The ones in San Agustín are delicious though can be extremely spicy. We can't wait to try them here.

For now, we wander down what seems to be the main street, cobbled and charming as anything you've ever seen, to the well-manicured town center. We're looking in the shops for silver jewelry for gifts but it's a little expensive. After meandering through various streets and alleys, admiring the hidden staircases and colorful houses, we decide it's time to eat. We head back up the main street, stopping to buy a yellow, wool poncho with an Aztec design around the neck and hood because it will make a beautiful decoration for our home, not only in San Agustín but in Portland as well. We also find a set of lapis and turquoise earrings for our grown-up child back in New York City; we figure they'll wear one, and their girlfriend the other.

It's hard to settle on a place for *pastes* but, when we do, we're glad we chose the one we did. We each have a cream of chicken variety and they are incredible. We decide to order some to go, but they only have one left, so we get that and another of chicken *tinga,* (kind of tangy tomato sauce). We figure we'll be hungry later. After that, we kind of feel like we've done everything there is to do here, so now we have to figure out how to get home. We would really prefer not to have to get back on the bus. We go back to where the taxi dropped us off, and there are a few waiting there, but no one knows where San Agustín is, and no one wants to take us. This is actually something we've encountered more than once in Mexico: the fact that people who live in fairly close proximity to our town have never heard of it, including the lady at the immigration office in Pachuca.

Finally, one driver talks to another, a youngish guy who seems to be up for it, but he doesn't know how to get there. People do, actually, have Google maps and Waze here, but even those apps can't always find San Agustín.

He does know how to get to Pachuca, of course, and I tell him I can guide him from there. Somewhere just north of Pachuca, he stops and picks up another guy, his dad, maybe, who helps him navigate though I'm perfectly capable of telling him how to get there. The ride is a little expensive, but within our budget for the day, and so we enjoy the luxury of not being on the bus, even if taking a cab means hurtling down the highway with no seatbelts and the wind blowing us to bits.

About an hour after we get home, I get a text from Rico asking if we want to go to Real del Monte tomorrow. It's uncanny. I apologize profusely for jumping the gun, since I knew he wanted to take us, but he takes it in stride, as he does with everything.

Today is the day all of San Agustín has been waiting for, El Festival de la Gordita! Yes, they dedicate an entire festival to the most popular food in San Agustín, the lowly *gordita*.

Every town and region has its specialties. In San Agustín it's the *gordita de panza de res*. If you recall, the *gordita* is kind of like a small pita made of corn meal, and stuffed with fillings. The *panza de res* is beef belly, the more fat the better, served with a spicy sauce. In Actopan the specialty is *barbacoa*, and in Pachuca and the surrounding mining towns it's the *paste*. Regional specialties, of course, can be found in all parts of Mexico, and you readers who have traveled in the country know what I'm talking about.

In reality, this festival is more of an excuse to have a huge party and to bring in visitors from around the region, all of it orchestrated by Arlo. I tell you, though only twenty-eight years of age, the man should run for mayor. He has performed a miracle. There is an entire schedule of events for today besides the eating of food: concerts and folkloric dances on the main stage set up on one side of the *centro*, a marionette troupe who will be performing throughout the day near the mercado, and artisans, selling their wares as far as the eye can see.

At 9:30 we catch the first set of folkloric dancers, children, who do their native dances with great enthusiasm. We spot Arlo and Fabricio, running around like maniacs, and wave to them. Around 10:30, we bring our laundry to the same-day lady on the outskirts of town, then we head back to the festival to partake of the main event. Don't get me wrong, there are all kinds of foods for sale, not just gorditas. You can get tacos and tamales and lots of other things, along a corridor covered with an enormous tent, which takes up the entire main street that runs along the east side of the *mercado* and the *centro*. On one side of this corridor is stand after stand of vendors cooking the *gorditas* and other foods to order while people crowd around, waiting their turn. On the other side are maybe fifty large round tables set up, surrounded by chairs, where you can sit and eat.

Jon and I order two *gorditas* each. I get both of *panza de res*, which we've never tried, and he gets one of the *panza* and one of *tinga*. After getting our food, we go to find a seat at a table, and wind up sitting with a family who has a couple of seats to spare. In the usual San Agustín way, we all strike up a conversation, and soon are chatting it up like old friends. There are bowls of sauce on the table which they urge us to slather onto our *gorditas*. It's spicy but so good. In fact, the *gorditas* are wonderful, but two is enough beef belly for me. A guy is selling freshly-squeezed orange and grapefruit juice, which is the perfect thing to go with the *gorditas* since, this is, after all, breakfast.

After that, we go back to the house to relax for a while, grateful that it's so close to the action. We see, now, why this festival, which is only the sixth ever, and which didn't happen at all during the pandemic, is so important to San Agustín. People have come from far and wide to take part and enjoy the food and activities, bringing a huge economic boon to the town. Some of them will likely stay the night (though there are only a few hotels), which will have them in town for the *tianguis* tomorrow, another opportunity to spend money.

After our break, we head back to the festival to check out the vendors of artisanal goods who have also come to town just for this occasion. There are certain acts I want to catch on the main stage as well, but the schedule is completely off, as the first act started really late and pushed the rest back by a couple of hours.

Meandering among the rows of vendors, which are set up on either side of the main street but farther down the block from the *centro,* keeps us entertained. We're happy to see this isn't just an opportunity for out-of-town vendors to make money because all the local shops have set up tables as well. There are gifts and gee-gaws and doo-dads, some run of the mill and other wonderful artisanal products: chocolates, cheeses, snacks of all kinds, coffee, tequila, *pulque* (a thick, alcoholic drink made from the agave plant), traditional clothing, hats, leather goods, jewelry, and more. Anna and her husband have their table set up just outside their shop with all their wonderful lotions and soaps, but I let others purchase their wares today as I can get them any time.

I've been keeping my eye out for an artisanal tablecloth to bring home to Portland, but no such luck today. Instead, I buy handmade truffles as a Christmas gift for my sister's husband, some snacks for us, a pair of sunglasses (definitely not artisanal), and Jon buys a homemade coffee liquor.

We enjoy more of the folkloric dances, now performed by professional dancers, and then pick up some *tacos dorados* to take home for dinner before we go to another of the main events happening today—or this evening actually—*la posada* at Anna's house.

Posada means "inn" in Spanish: in this case, the inns from which Mary and Joseph were turned away when looking for shelter. I participated in *las posadas* in Tucson when I was young but, here, they do it differently as I find out once we head over to Anna's, about a fifteen-minute walk from our place into a nearby neighborhood. According to my fitness band, this puts us at about 15,000 steps today.

We get there at 7:00, the appointed time, and are guided to sit in some chairs set up in the enclosed carport area of her grandparents' house, which is right next-door to where Anna lives with her husband, baby, sister, and parents. After fifteen minutes or so, there's a commotion in the street, and the sound of singing alerts us that the "pilgrims" are approaching. This is a group of neighbors, bearing the icons of Mary and Joseph in a glass box. Once they arrive at the door, they sing a song, asking to be let in for shelter. We, on the inside, respond in song, that they may not enter. This goes back and forth for a while, until they finally "convince" us to let them in. This is a moment of great celebration, met with prayers and more songs. The pilgrims come in and set the image of Mary and Joseph by the Christmas tree that adorns the carport, in a kind of nativity scene, or *crèche,* that the family has arranged beneath the tree. What is missing from the nativity is Jesus himself, but he won't be added until Christmas Eve at midnight.

After the singing is done, all the guests, which include the pilgrims, are served tamales, pozole, and punch. The tamales that

Anna's mom has made are of chicken and green *tomatillo* sauce, the most delicious tamales I've ever had. There are even chocolate ones for dessert! By now it's about 8:00, and we've had a long day of walking and celebrating and eating, so Anna's husband offers us a ride home, which we gratefully accept, along with many more tamales. When we get home, I put them in the freezer, to serve for Christmas Eve when my family will be here, in just a week's time. Since my dad grew up in Tucson, and we moved there when I was thirteen, our family is very steeped in the Christmas traditions of the desert southwest, and that includes eating Mexican food every Christmas Eve, especially tamales. As we're going to be spending Christmas deep in the heart of Mexico this year, we will certainly continue this tradition with enthusiasm!

From Jon: Sadly, the coffee liquor had gone sour by the time I opened it the next day. Oh well. It is taking some time to get used to the fact that, for example, the planned events of the festival happened on a timeframe of their own, no matter what the original schedule might actually have been. This is a culture that sees time as more fluid than structured. With big events like the Gordita Festival, it's perhaps more noticeable than when it occurs in smaller less impactful ways in daily life. It is not at all unusual to meet a friend on the sidewalk and stop to speak with them for an undetermined amount of time. It doesn't matter if one is on the way to do some leisurely window-shopping or if you're trying to keep an appointment with the dentist. That moment on the street is the most important moment there is. As Americans, it's easy to feel annoyed by this but, as humans, it's just as easy to appreciate a culture that values such small moments over the strictures of any clock.

1,400,000 to 1,450,000 Steps

Today is the day of the UPFIM Christmas Party. School officially let out last week, as it's now the 19th of December, but there really haven't been classes at all for about two weeks—at least for me.

Still, this party seems like it will be a big deal, though it starts a little late for me, close to 9:00 p.m. I know, I know, I'm very old and boring, but I'm used to going to bed at around 9:30, in particular here in San Agustín because the sun comes blasting through the windows in Jon's office area by 7:00, even though we finally have curtains for them. However, we couldn't cover all the windows since we have to open one section to light the boiler every morning, which is just outside the upstairs windows. And remember, there's an interior window opening from that room into our bedroom, which we've partially covered with the big, ugly clothes cabinet that Marco left in the house, but the light still comes in. And if that doesn't wake us up, Chula barking just before her first morning poop will do it. If that doesn't happen, someone is bound to be setting off fireworks at 6:00 a.m. to celebrate some saint day or another.

Honestly, I'm not complaining—well, maybe a little bit—because the culture is the culture and we're here to learn about and celebrate it. Also, Mexico is Mexico, complete with funkily-designed houses and barking dogs, and I love it, we love it, no matter what.

Anyway, I don't have the perfect thing to wear to this party, which all the employees at the school will attend, from the cleaning people to the rector. I do have a pretty, silky teal-colored dress that I wore to the cocktail party COMEXUS threw for us in Mexico City, but it's not very warm. Ultimately, I put on a light-weight sweater under the dress, plus tights, and some boots I bought here that are a little chunky for this particular dress, but they'll do. Over that, I wear my winter coat that I brought from Portland. Jon has some nice slacks, a button-down shirt, and a tie. It's going to have to do.

Rico picks us up for the party at about 8:30, and we arrive at the event space in the one and only modern, upscale hotel in Actopan just before 9:00. We sit at the table with Frank and others, some of whom we know. I'm expecting Cristina to arrive at any moment.

At precisely nine, dinner is served: a Waldorf salad to start, followed by a square of lasagna, and, after that, medallions of pork with a pomegranate sauce and mashed potatoes. It's good, but very American, which surprises me. There's nary a tortilla in sight! I'm thinking to myself that this is a very heavy dinner to be eating so late at night but I eat it all because I'm hungry.

While we're dining, the band starts, a Cumbia band with a sexy, female lead singer. If you don't know what Cumbia is, check this out https://rb.gy/p3bonw. I tend to like Cumbia because it's sort of hypnotic though I suppose some might identify that same quality as tedious. In general, it's very popular dance music in Mexico and the band is good.

No one hits the dance floor while we're eating, but eventually, one couple, very good dancers, makes their way, and little by little, others follow. I'm feeling a little nervous to get up and dance, at least until the dance floor is full because we don't know the steps. Yet, I realize we can actually swing dance to this music because it has a 4/4 beat. You can dance swing to anything with a 4/4 beat. Jon and I brave it and end up nailing it. Everybody is impressed—wowed even—and I feel vindicated, though for what, I'm not sure. Maybe it's because we've shown them that we Americans have dance skills too and that we don't have to know the Mexican dances to burn it up to their music.

When the band takes a break, they pipe in recorded music of a more general nature—Mexican pop music, essentially—and now people really flood the dance floor. We do this type of circle dance with repetitive moves that are easy to pick up, and I grab my teacher friends, Irene and another woman I love teaching with, Antonia, and pull them onto the dance floor. Jon sits this part out, but I enthusiastically join in until I finally poop out. Now I see why a big meal is served before the dancing—you need the energy. Dessert has been served, but since I'm not sure what kind of sugar is used in it, I skip it. We hang out and chat with Rico and others until around 11:00. Cristina hasn't shown up. I text her to see if she's coming, but she says she's busy with a paper. I have the feeling this isn't really her cup of tea, besides the fact that I think she and others are still mad at the administration.

Rico offers to take us home, but we won't hear of it since he's clearly having a good time and, besides, has maybe had a bit to drink. Somebody calls for a cab, but it's going to take them a long time to get there (remember, no Ubers). So, finally, we compromise, and Rico takes us to the taxi stand which is not too far away. We get home about midnight, shockingly late for us, but worth it.

1,450,000 to 1,520,000 Steps

My 90-year-old mother, my sister, Susan, her husband, John, and his sister have arrived. It's funny how we don't have a word in English for the sister or brother of your sister or brother-in-law, but in Spanish we do: *concuño* or *concuña*, although, when I went to double check the spelling, it seems it's very colloquial and not in use in other countries. Anyway, my *concuña*, whom I never met before, is named Carol.

The group flew in from Tijuana, just across the border from where my sister lives in San Diego, and arrived in Mexico City at about 6:00 a.m. I figured that, for sure, by the time they got their luggage and went through customs, then dealt with traffic in Mexico City and drove the two hours from there to here, it would be at least 10:00 by the time they got there. But, nope! I'm still in my jammies at 9:00 when I get a text from Susan saying they're here! She hired a fancy SUV to transport all of them and their luggage from the airport. Since my mom has a little trouble walking, and my brother-in-law as well, being an amputee, she wanted to make sure they were as comfortable as possible. Not only that, but, clearly, that driver is speedy.

It's wonderful to see them. I am truly gratified that Susan had the idea of coming to us for Christmas because it makes me feel like, not only do she and the others care about spending Christmas with us, but they care about this experience we're having and want to share it with us. Of course, we love San Agustín so much by this point we're thrilled to be able to share it with them as well.

The plumbing disaster unfolds immediately after they arrive, but I won't go into that again. Welcome to San Agustín! Instead, since we know it gets resolved this very day, let's fast forward to dinner tonight at La Hacienda. I knew this was going to be the place for their first dinner in town because I wanted that dinner to be as nice as possible and, of course, La Hacienda is really the only place for that. We're accommodated at the best table, and the owner, José, goes out of his way to make sure we have everything we need, and even brings a gas heater over by the table since the restaurant is partially open to the elements and not heated overall—like pretty much everywhere else in San Agustín.

I'm particularly glad to see that my brother-in-law loves it because he can be a bit picky. Everyone's able to have a sangria or beer or whatever they choose to drink (for some reason they don't offer wine), and a delicious meal.

Afterwards, we call a cab (only possible because I happen to have the number of a driver in San Agustín on my phone) and get my mom back to our house and everyone else to their hotel. In fact, I figure John and my mom will be covering most distances via cab—a simple alternative to trying to have them walk on the uneven and broken sidewalks.

Today is Christmas Eve, and the hotel folks have come over for breakfast, for the specialty that Jon has "invented," an egg cooked on top of a lightly fried tortilla with cheese or whatever is handy, appropriately named by a friend of ours, the *Juan Taco*. After that, Susan and Carol spend the morning exploring the town and the marketplace, which, as is typical when there's a holiday coming up, has expanded to take up a good portion of the *centro*, with specialty fruits and vegetables, gift items, sweets, Christmas decorations, etc. I even manage to get my mom to walk the two blocks to the *centro* to take in the action. I just can't have her miss it; it's so incredibly festive at the moment with hordes of people snapping up their last minute necessities for this evening and tomorrow.

Since it's been a few hours since breakfast, we're hungry again, and, though we'd like the others to join us, they're still involved with their exploration, so mom, Jon, and I stop into a little breakfast place that has opened up on our street—only on the weekends, and only until noon—for some pancakes, enchiladas, and grilled cheese toast. By the way, enchiladas are a breakfast/lunch food in Mexico, as are *chilaquiles*, a wondrous kind of thick soup with triangles of fried tortillas in red or green sauce, cheese, and chicken on top if you request it.

John is chilling at the hotel, where he can hang out in the bar (though he doesn't drink) and watch sports on the television there while sipping alcohol-free beer.

Finally, we gather in the evening at my place for dinner. I'm thrilled to hear how Susan and Carol have taken to San Agustín. They get the charm of it one hundred percent. I'm so relieved because I wondered if it was just me and Jon who felt that way. Clearly not. They get it, my mom gets it, and even John, who tends to prefer a more resort type of vibe, gets it.

I picked up our favorite *tacos dorados* from the marketplace earlier in the day and have warmed them up for dinner to go with Jon's special guacamole, along with the tamales left over from Angie's posada. We then gather on the couch, which is big enough for everyone, bundled up in every blanket in the house, and my sister reads a Christmas story to us. This is a tradition she started when her daughter was little, and continues to this day though all the kids in our family have grown up. We adults still love it though. She always chooses the perfect story, and this time it's a Mexican tale, the legend of the Poinsettia flower, which in Mexico they call the Christmas Eve Flower, or *Flor de Nochebuena*. Trust me, by the end, it has all of us in tears, which her stories usually do.

At around nine, I go to call the cab driver to take the three of them back to the hotel, but he doesn't answer. I guess that makes sense on Christmas Eve. So Jon and I put on our coats and head to the *centro,* where the taxi stand is, to see if we can hail one there. No such luck. In fact, there isn't a taxi in sight. Walking back past the church, we see people leaving there with babies in their arms. How random is that? We wonder at the strangeness of literally everyone carrying a baby. It is only on closer inspection that we ascertain that those are not babies, but rather baby dolls nestled in their arms. This tradition, I understand, is so that they can have their baby Jesuses blessed for their nativity scenes.

I'm thinking John will have to spend the night at our house, as the two women are perfectly capable of walking back to the hotel, but he decides he can do it, and sets off with his female escorts to cover the five or so blocks. They text us about twenty minutes later to report that he made it, no problem. This is a relief since I figure we won't find a cab in the morning either.

This morning, everyone sleeps in, and we schedule brunch at our house for around noon. I've baked a blueberry coffeecake for the occasion, and whip up some bacon and eggs to go with it. Our Christmas tree is looking adorable, decorated with lots of ornaments we've gathered over the last week or so, and surrounded by the gifts that everyone has set at its base in anticipation of Christmas morning. We've agreed the gifts would be small and inexpensive, as spending Christmas in Mexico together is the true gift.

When the folks from the hotel arrive, we settle back on the couch and get to opening our gifts. As we requested, my mom and sister gave us organic chocolate since we can't find that here in San Agustín. Carol has brought us a welcome mat she found in San Agustín that says *Bienvenido,* as we didn't have one in front of the door. Susan has delivered gifts from my child and their partner—ones they had sent to her from New York—hand designed by my child's partner: T-shirts with San Agustín written across the front and an image of the town church, done in the unique and beautiful way only she can do. I had commissioned one for Jon, but she made one for me too, which is a lovely surprise. Susan also delivered to me the other gift I ordered for Jon and had sent to San Diego for her to bring: a new Killer's t-shirt, exactly like the one the laundromat had lost.

Jon gives me a gift I was expecting, but has turned out more beautifully than I could have hoped, a small gold pendant shaped like a sunflower, which we'd commissioned the only jeweler in town to make. It's to go on the gold chain Jon gave me a year ago, which I've been wearing plain, waiting until I found the perfect thing to go on it. This sunflower is it: a representation of one of the crops they grow in abundance here in the Valle del Mezquital, and one of my favorite flowers, something to always remind me of this amazing place.

We give the women gifts from Anna's shop: handmade lotions, soaps, shampoo bars, and body scrubs, and John gets the artisanal chocolate truffles we bought at the Gordita Festival.

After that we eat brunch, and eventually the others either retire to the hotel or go to wander through the *tianguis*, as it is, after all, Sunday, and the *tianguis* doesn't stop for anything, not even Christmas.

Again, we bring my mom out to see it because I can't let her miss this marvel. We don't venture far in, but far enough for her to experience the sights and sounds, the sheer Mexican-ness of this phenomenon which, to me, never having been to one in any other town, is the essence of San Agustín.

For dinner tonight I've defrosted the abundant stuffing from Thanksgiving, purchased two of the roasted chickens, made the *calabacitas* and mashed potatoes, and another apple crumble for dessert—pretty much a mirror of the Thanksgiving feast. Everyone has helped decorate the table and it's as festive a Christmas dinner as I've ever seen. They all love the food, and I feel warm and happy, basking in the love brought from this portion of my family who traveled far and intrepidly to spend this holiday with us. The best Christmas present ever.

From Jon: the displays of goods for sale at the tianguis are incredible. There are so many things to see and possibly purchase its fairly difficult to take in everything. Still, one of the offerings that caught my attention are large super colorful displays of candies. Actually, side-by-side with the candies, in wrappers just as colorful, are cohetes *(fireworks). There are all sorts, from sparklers to M80s being sold to anyone with a coin or two. There are no warning labels nor instructions of any kind other than on the candies which tell you they contain* exceso de azúcar, *'cause you know, too much sugar is bad for you. It's fair to point out in this moment that while all snack items in Mexico are strictly labeled with clear warnings of their effect on one's health, there are literally no alternative snack options available anywhere. Your 8-year-old might be wounded by a malfunctioning high explosive, purchased for 10 pesos along with a lime sucker, but, when in the hospital, the doctors will not be having to deal with his excessive intake of sugar or salt because they know those warnings are in place. To be clear, I'm not indicating that such disparities do not occur in the US: there are laws that restrict kids from buying cigarettes until they're 21, but they can buy an assault rifle at 18. Go figure.*

1,520,000 to 1,600,000 Steps

Today I want the family to see the university. I'm sure there will be taxis, now that we're past Christmas, to take my mom and brother-in-law, whom I will accompany so I can point out the buildings where I teach, etc. Jon, Susan, and Carol are up for the walk, though it's a long one, but they can always take a combi back.

Once again, I can't get a taxi driver by phone. Has everyone taken the week off? Mom and John say they can walk to the *centro* so we can grab a cab there. We make it that far with no problem, but there are no cabs in sight. We now only have one option, and that's to take a combi, though the stop is about a block further. I'm worried about them getting into the vehicle because it's a high, and very narrow, step up. I've clearly underestimated them, however, because they both gamely hop (well not exactly hop) into the combi and we make ourselves as comfortable as possible on the bench seats. Fortunately, there are not very many people riding it today, as it's not a school day. I figure we'll go as far as UPFIM, get off, and then get another one back.

I love this road to UPFIM. As you get to the outskirts of San Agustín, just a few minutes out, you pass beautiful fields of corn, yellowing now at this time of year, and green alfalfa, with the blue/grey hills in the distance. Once you get past the one stoplight along the way, the road is lined with cypress trees. The first glimpse of the university is of the sports center, then you can see Docencia 2 in the distance, and finally you come upon the entrance from which, if you look hard enough, you can see the library and Docencia 1. You can also spot the communist buildings from here, gayly decorated with

Christmas ornaments. The mural of the famous communists is nearly obliterated by a giant Christmas tree.

I'm pointing all this out to my mom and John when it occurs to me that, if we just stay on the combi, the driver will continue his route and circle back past the uni again, and return us to San Agustín. I ask him if that's okay and, of course, he's fine with it, we'll just have to pay the round trip fare which is all of twenty pesos each.

We head past UPFIM and into Los Filtros, just a few houses and little shops, yet another view of Mexico that my passengers haven't seen. Just as for me, Mexico is endlessly fascinating to them. They've both spent a fair amount of time in the country on other occasions, but this is a side of it they haven't seen much of: rural and rustic and real. The driver continues up towards the hills and the road turns to dirt. It's a bumpy ride, past farms with chickens and goats, more or less in the area where Jon and I went to the baptism party with Arlo and Fabricio. Along the way, the driver is pointing things out to us, especially the fancy houses way up in the hills, some of which, he says, are owned by rich Americans though we've seen nary a one of them in town. As it turns out, the driver is a great tour guide.

Finally, we head back toward the university, along the smelly canal, and my guests get to glimpse UPFIM again. By the time we get back to town, it's been about a 45 minutes ride to an area they would never have gotten to see if we'd merely taken a cab. I feel bad that the others didn't get to take this little trip because it certainly was a unique experience, and mom and John are thrilled they got to have it.

After the ride, John goes back to the hotel which is much closer to the combi stop than my house and, apparently, Susan and Carol have gone there too. I take mom, slowly, back to the house. Arlo and Fabricio are coming for dinner tonight, so I head back out to the *paste* shop to get a supply for dinner. One of my goals of this family visit is to not spend the whole time cooking since everyone loves Mexican food and wants to sample it all anyway. I get two *pastes* a piece, but have decided that they will be too spicy for anyone but Arlo and Fabricio, so I take the stuffing out of about half of them, and refill them with a tuna and mayo mixture, which I've done before and is actually really good. This process, however, takes me more time than I thought it would so here I am, spending time cooking after all. Anyway, after that's done, I heat them up in the oven while preparing a salad to go with it. Keep in mind that preparing any vegetables, raw or cooked, requires disinfecting them first by soaking them in a water and a Microdyne (iodine) bath.

The dinner goes really well because, of course, Arlo and Fabricio are the most charming guests ever. Fabricio doesn't speak much English but he does understand a lot, so I don't have to do much translating. We have the leftover cobbler for dessert and Arlo takes some home because he adores it.

This morning we're hosting Anna and her family for brunch. I've prepared a *strata* per my sister's suggestion, kind of a big, crustless quiche made from eggs, onions, mushrooms, chorizo, and cheese, which somewhat sticks to my less than ideal pan. Jon has gone to the bakery to get a variety of pastries to go with it. Anna's dad isn't in attendance, but her mom, sister, husband, and of course their baby is. They are the most delightful family, as I've mentioned, and the baby is the cutest thing I've ever seen, with the exception of my own now grown child. Anna's husband speaks English quite well, and the conversation flows in both languages.

I've been trying to figure out how to get us to Tula tomorrow, because that's going to be the big excursion of this visit. I haven't come up with any solution but hiring two taxis...if I can find them. The problem with that is that, once the taxis get us there, they're not going to wait around, and I don't know if we can get transportation back to San Agustín. I don't want to take any chances that we'll be stranded because I'm not going to be able to get everyone to the bus stop, which is a fairly long walk from the archeological site.

However, Anna's mom knows of a company that hires out private combis that you can pay to take you anywhere you want, and they'll wait for you and bring you back. This sounds like the perfect solution so I text the number she gives me. It turns out that for sixty bucks I can reserve the combi, which will pick us up at the house in the morning and then pass by the hotel to get the others.

This afternoon, after Anna's family leaves, we've planned to go to Actopan so my group can see the convent. This is going to require two taxis which, fortunately, I'm able to book. We get to Actopan about 4:00, tour the convent, and buy some souvenirs from nearby vendors. As we're about to leave to go have dinner, we're approached by two tiny girls selling *chicle* (gum). They can't be more than seven, out in the plaza all by themselves. Their faces are grimy and their clothes ragged. The look at me, my mom, and Carol, with our fair hair and blue eyes, like they've never seen anything like us in their lives. In Spanish, I tell them we're from the United States but they've never heard of it. I tell them we're living in San Agustín, which is only a half an hour away, but they've never heard of it either. I can tell by their bright eyes that they're smart. I think, if only they could have an education it'd likely go a long ways toward improving their lot in life. I'm sure they don't go to school though, and probably never will. I'm also sure that selling gum is vital to the livelihoods of their families, which makes me wonder where their adults are. Is anyone looking out for them, seeing that they don't get abducted? They could so easily be grabbed and taken away to be trafficked. I fear for them, I really do, and my mom comments that, if she could, she'd take them to the U.S. with her and give them a life with opportunity. But, of course, she can't. There's nothing any of us can do but give them some pesos, let them keep the gum, and show them kindness.

They are so sweet, so curious. I wish them to somehow escape this poverty they are mired in.

Jon wonders if it's an act, to get tourists to shell out money, but I think this is very jaded of him. And even if it is, they're still having to resort to such extremes to earn a few pennies.

Like the rich Americans we are, we head off to dinner in the same place we went for my birthday, a spot where everyone can get the meal and cocktails they desire.

From Jon: My thought that the whole thing might be an act was most certainly jaded. Geo was correct in this. However, I feel the need to point out that my attitude stems not from living here in Mexico, but rather from living in the US, where so many things are designed purely with the intent of separating the unsuspecting from their money. Also, to my privileged senses, it boggles the mind that what we were seeing could be real, that these children were exactly what they seemed to be, innocent, impoverished, and completely unaware of a world outside of their own immediate environment. How can it be that they live without the multiplicity of modern conveniences that I take for granted and complain about when I do not have access? Let's face it, I had to arrange for a cappuccino machine to be delivered to this place where there is only a coffee-like beverage I've declared undrinkable. Back in Portland, we're a long way from wealthy yet, comparatively, I am a child of untold riches, attempting to make sense of what actual poverty really looks like. At this point, looking back, I've come around to see that I am, indeed, something from another universe, trying to understand where I've landed. Those children and the situation they live in is real. My empathy for them is palpable, yet all we've been able to offer are a few pesos and a wish for a brighter future.

We have gone ahead and hired the combi for our trip to Tula today, and the driver shows up on time to scoop up me, Jon, and mom, and then we head over to the hotel to get the rest of the gang. The combi is very comfortable, almost plush, with plenty of room for everyone. I ask the driver if he'd be available to take the family to the airport tomorrow because Susan has hired another fancy SUV to transport them, and it's very expensive. He says yes and quotes us a price which is half that of the SUV. Susan is delighted and cancels the other ride.

We get to Tula around 10:30 and the driver is prepared to wait. I tell him to give us two hours, and admonish the group we can't take more time than that, or we'll owe him for another hour beyond the time it will take to drive us home.

For most people, exploring Tula in two hours is plenty, but we have two folks who are challenged walkers and there are no wheelchairs or handicapped accessible anything. I even checked ahead of time to be sure. You'd think they'd provide little carts for a fee, with drivers to tour people around the site, an obvious extra source of money, but nothing like that exists. It's a shame that only the relatively able-bodied get to enjoy this wondrous place. I've been worried that my mom and John wouldn't be able to do the one-mile round trip walk, not to mention the extra quarter of a mile or so required to meander around the site, even in the most limited way, but now I've seen John can more than handle it. My mom, not so much. I actually tried to discourage her from going on this trip and offered to stay home with her, but she wouldn't hear of it. The woman is nothing if not determined.

I refuse the tour guide this time because I feel Jon and I have enough information, thanks to Cristina, to intelligently talk about the history of the place. Once we make it along the path and through the gamut of *tchotchke* vendors (*tchotchke* is not a Spanish or native word, but a Yiddish one that serves to describe such touristy items so well), I get to experience the satisfaction of seeing my family members' faces as they glimpse for the first time the pyramid with the warrior statues on top, nobly guarding the ancient city. Mom and I head straight there because I know she won't have the energy to wander around the rest of the ruins, but I point them out to her on the way and explain the history. She, of course, can't climb to the top of the pyramid, but can see the statues quite well from the base. Susan, Carol, and Jon scramble to the top like monkeys but I stay with mom and point out the other features of the site that we can see from there, sharing the information I know about it.

After about an hour and a half, I let the others know we've got to head back. I get going with mom, this time with Jon on the other side of her to help support her. It's really slow going. I can feel her wanting to give up more than once, but there's no other way to get back to the combi without walking. There's no other transport, no one to carry her, nothing but her own two feet. We're in sight of the information center when she really begins to lag. I'm urging her on, encouraging her with everything I've got, telling her it's just a few more steps, just a few more. We finally make it and she sits on a low wall to rest, but now we've just got five minutes until 12:30 so I make her get up, and we walk another few hundred feet, down several short flights of stairs, and finally get her into the combi where the driver has the AC running and Susan and I have snacks and water for everyone.

My mom is so proud of herself that she made this little journey, and thrilled to have seen such a magnificent place. She says she wouldn't have missed it for the world and I'm so glad she didn't have to.

We have the driver deposit the others at the hotel when we get back to San Agustín. When we arrive at the house, I plop mom onto the couch where she passes out asleep. I'm scared that we've overdone it—that it's been too much for her—and even have a moment of fear that she won't wake up from her nap. But that's ridiculous. She's up and at 'em two hours later, full of energy.

Everyone comes over in the evening for dinner. I'd originally planned for us to eat tacos *al pastor* (pronounced "ahl-pah-STORE"), delicious soft corn tortillas with roasted seasoned pork and pineapple, a Mexican staple, at our favorite little *taquería* called Los Volcanes. It's far though, just at the edge of San Agustín on the road that leads to the university, and would require more taxis to get us there (at least for those who can't walk it). So, I decide to go get the food myself and bring it home. My plan is to buy the meat from Los Volcanes, where they sell it by the pound, and get fresh tortillas from our favorite *tortillería* to go with it.

I get to Los Volcanes around 5:30, knowing they sometimes don't open in earnest until 6:00 (an anomaly in San Agustín). They don't have any *pastor* meat ready. Of course, I'm starving at this point, and get one taco, with the small amount they have left over from the night before, to hold me over. I decide we have enough leftover roasted chicken at home to make tacos with—that is—if I can get the tortillas. But I know the *tortillería* closes at 6:00 on the dot. It's now 5:45 and it's a good fifteen-minute walk back into town.

I high-tail it, and hear the church clock strike 6:00 as I'm just a block away. I race to the *tortillería* and get there just before they close the doors. They're not making any more tortillas, but I ask if they have any leftovers. They do, thank God, and I'm able to get a kilo's worth. I grab a couple of avocados from the one stand that tends to be open later than the mercado itself, and get home to a house full of hungry folks. I apologize that I couldn't get the *pastor* meat, but they're undaunted. There's not as much leftover chicken as I thought, but there's still stuffing, and we make ourselves some unconventional tacos out of it all, along with Jon's guacamole. Everyone ends up satisfied. Besides, the "leftover" tortillas are so amazing they're the star of the show.

This morning the family heads back on their hired combi to the airport in Mexico City. The visit has been too short, but packed full of great moments. It's definitely been an incredible Christmas holiday with them, one I'll never forget.

1,600,000 to 1,780,000 Steps

We get one evening to chill after all our visitors leave, and then another arrives, a young woman from Fulbright, one of my fellow ETAs. This person, Gwen, is all of about 21 years old, but someone I've befriended simply through our ETA WhatsApp chat thread. This thread has been a lifeline for me and many others as we maneuver through this year. Some people have had some really big challenges, so big, that a couple of them have chosen to cut the grant short and go home. That would never be an option for me—partly because I am loving this experience, but also, I want full credit for completing my Fulbright grant. I want to forever be able to say I'm a Fulbrighter! Yet, one person left because her gastrointestinal system simply couldn't handle Mexico. I get that. God knows Jon and I have been through our fair share of stomach issues. Another person left because...well, I don't know. Maybe she was lonely or maybe she was just too dang cold. She was, after all, placed in a mountain town in Hidalgo, higher, I think, than Real del Monte, so like 9,000 feet. I remember her saying it was freezing in September. I can only imagine how it is now, in December. Poor thing. Others have commented that it's so hot and humid where they are that their clothes are constantly damp with sweat. Eww. Again, I reiterate how glad I am not to have been placed somewhere steamy.

One person I know of was threatened on the streets of his town—either because he's gay or Asian. This threw him so badly he asked to be transferred. His request was granted and now he's happy. Other people didn't start teaching until late in October because their institutions were on strike. Others have ended up in the hospital with various maladies, usually stomach related.

Then there's the money issue, which I haven't really spoken about. We Fulbrighters in Mexico receive a pretty small scholarship compared to some who go to other countries. This is because Mexico is a poor country. Though Fulbright is partially funded by the U.S. State Department, the commission in each individual country is also responsible for contributing funds. In our case, the Mexican Secretary of Public Education (SEP) funds our grants. And since they don't have a lot of money, we don't get that much either. Fulbright warned us about this ahead of time, letting us know when we applied that we would probably need to have some savings or other sources of income flowing from the U.S. to see us through the year. In my case, I have the financial resources I've already mentioned. That's enough to keep us comfortable here, along with the scholarship payments. However, the payment we were supposed to receive at the end of October was a week late and that put a lot of the ETAs who had rent to pay at that time in a bad position. The chat really blew up over that issue because many of them were angry about being put in such a compromised position financially. Not only that, but they ended up not having money to celebrate Day of the Dead with, and that's a pity. I remember one person commented they had exactly 80 pesos in their bank account to last them a week. Folks were actually worried about where their next meal was coming from which is absolutely unacceptable in a prestigious program like this.

Gwen was one of those people. Of course, younger people, regardless of being told to have savings set aside or whatever, are much more likely to find themselves in a challenging position economically. I helped to talk some of these people through it at that time, including Gwen. Having made a close connection with her, she wanted to come to San Agustín to see me and meet Jon, which I thought was sweet.

She treks here today on the bus from Puebla. We meet her at the bus stop when she arrives, bring her home, feed her, spend time chatting about all the things we have in common that we love, notably, books, movies, and music, then we go out to tour around San Agustín, and ultimately end up at Los Volcanes for *tacos al pastor*.

She is, as it turns out, is an incredibly talented singer and shares some of her videos with us. You cannot believe what a beautiful and powerful voice this small woman has.

Today, New Year's Eve, I make her French toast for breakfast, and then she leaves on the 11:00 bus. Not a long stay but a meaningful one. I feel I've made a lifelong friend in this young person and I look forward to seeing her at our midterm reunion which will take place from January 9th to the 13th in La Paz.

In fact, seeing Gwen there, and a few others I've gotten close with through the chat, or that I really connected with during the orientation in Mexico City, is pretty much the only thing I'm looking forward to about it. I just don't want to leave San Agustín. It's not that I don't want to leave Jon for the five days. He can fend for himself quite well. I literally don't want to leave my wonderful little town here. Sure, it will be cool to be at the beach and experience a different part of Mexico, but I don't want to have to get myself to Mexico City, get on a plane and spend four days in meetings, when I could be here roaming around my town and enjoying the life we've come to love so much. Gwen feels the same way about her town, Puebla. Though it will be great to see the other ETAs, four days of meetings is too much for anyone.

As the day wears on, clouds roll in along with the cold. We don't have anything planned for tonight; we've had enough excitement over the last week. So, as we sit and watch Netflix on my computer, as cozy as we can be with our two space heaters and lots of blankets, a storm develops complete with wild thunder, lightning, and pouring rain. Kind of a fitting way to end this spectacular year.

This morning, January 1st, we get some sad news. Little Gorda, the pug, has passed away. Apparently, the gate was left open and

Gorda ran out and got hit by a car. I feel terrible for the family and for Chula the Akita. You can see how lonely she is without her little friend.

Though it's a sad way to start the year, it's *tianguis* day, the sun is out, and there's definitely a feeling of hope in the air.

School is still out but, though it starts up again next week, I won't be there because I'll be going to La Paz, a thing I still haven't really reconciled myself to. COMEXUS is flying everyone there, and we'll be staying at a nice hotel on the water, but I just can't get excited about it. Not only that, but I'm nervous about the presentation I'll be giving during the course of the reunion. Everyone has to prepare a five-minute presentation, preferably PowerPoint, in Spanish, about our experience so far in Mexico. It can be about our teaching, or about friends we've met, food we like, the culture, anything, really, that shows off what we've been doing during the four and a half months we've been here so far.

In my usual hyper-organized way (I wasn't always so organized but my master's program made me that way) I had my presentation finished well in advance and, now, practice it on a regular basis. I even did it for my family while they were here. It's called *"Mujeres extraordinarias"* (Extraordinary Women) and is about the amazing women I've met here and how they have impacted or inspired me. I've chosen six: Cristina, Anna, Maria (Marco's mom), my hair dresser Isabel, my neighbor Miriam, and a young woman I've been working with virtually on a writing project, who lives in the state of Tlaxcala.

Side note from Georgina: you'll notice that I didn't capitalize the "e" in extraordinarias. *That is because titles of things: books, movies, etc., don't get capitalized beyond the first word in Spanish. Also, words like days of the week, months, languages, and nationalities don't get capitalized. Other names and proper nouns are mostly the same as English.*

Although I was an actress for twenty years, I get nervous speaking in front of a large group, and we'll be about seventy in La Paz. Doing the presentation is Spanish doesn't help, though there's no reason I should be worried about it. I just don't want to make any major flubs. So, I've practiced and practiced until I nearly have everything memorized.

It's January 6th today, otherwise known as Three Kings Day in most Latin American countries, or Epiphany in other Christian traditions. It's the day that celebrates the arrival in Jerusalem of the three wise men, bringing gifts to the baby Jesus. Here in Mexico, it's essentially a day devoted to children. There are yet more stalls set up selling toys, and a mini-fair, with rides, and characters in costume representing the three kings. More than anything though, are *Rosca de Reyes*, a special cake-like bread, or bread-like cake, for sale as far as the eye can see. Bakeries are selling them, people with tables in the *centro* are selling them, stores that never sell baked goods are selling them—in short, everyone is selling them which makes me wonder who's buying them. Clearly, someone must be. We don't buy one because they're huge and when are we going to eat it? That kind of bread/cake doesn't generally appeal to us anyway. I only know about one tradition related to eating cake on this day, also known as Twelfth Night because it's twelve days after Christmas, wherein a bean or small doll is baked inside a cake and, once it's cut, the person who gets the bean or doll is named king or queen for the night, and gets to assign tasks to everyone else in the family or party.

I'm wondering if the tradition is the same here. As we pass by Cafée Rinkon, on our way back from a stroll on the plaza, we see that they also have the *Rosca de Reyes* for sale, baked by Maria, who is a phenomenal, professional baker. Fernando and Marco's waitress/girlfriend are manning the sales table, so we stop and chat. Fernando explains that, in their tradition, five or six little dolls are hidden in the cake, and whoever gets one has to perform a silly task.

This conversation comes up in the ETA chat and Gwen informs me that, where she is in Puebla, the tradition is that whoever gets the doll has to bring everyone (who everyone is, I don't know) tamales on February 2nd. Others confirm this, so maybe what Fernando told me is particular to his family's tradition.

Anyway, Jon and I head home and we've just settled in when the doorbell on the outside gate rings. Usually, if Miriam is home, she'll answer it, but their house is dark so I figure they're not around. I go to answer the bell and find some people in a car, just in front of the house, about to drive off. I ask who they're looking for and they want to know if the baker (referring to Miriam, who also is a talented pastry chef) has *Rosca* for sale. It's about 8:00 by now, so maybe the *Rosca* sellers in the *centro* have closed down for the night. Or, it's possible they're looking for the best possible *Rosca*, and figure Miriam would have it. I can see that Cafée Rinkon is still open, so I point them there, telling them that the *Rosca* is excellent. I actually have no idea if it is but, I figure, if Maria made it, it must be. They drive happily away toward the café, and I close the gate, pleased that not only do I now know what *Rosca* is, which I didn't at the beginning of the day, but I also know where to find the good stuff. I feel like a real local now.

1,780,000 to 1,850,000 Steps

Today, I'm off to La Paz. My flight doesn't leave until 3:00, then it's a 2 hour, non-stop trip. I call Antonio, the taxi driver who took us home from the Christmas party, and he picks me up just fifteen minutes late, and drives me all the way to the airport in Mexico City. This is a splurge—about 100 bucks in American money—but there's no way I'm slogging it on the bus to Pachuca, then on another bus to Mexico City. It's just too much to bear for a trip I don't want to take anyway. Antonio is a really nice guy and gets me there in good time. When I arrive, I immediately run into a gang of other ETAs taking the same flight, some of whom I know fairly well, not only from the WhatsApp chat but from our time together at orientation.

The plane is delayed about an hour, during which time I come to find out they don't have a seat for me. I have no idea why this is. I did check in ahead of time, but maybe not far enough ahead of time. One other person, a movie-star-good-looking ETA named Zeke is in the same boat. Finally, we're called to board the plane, and Zeke and I are told to wait by the boarding desk to find out if there are seats for us. If not, we'll be taking a plane to Cabo San Lucas and spending the night God knows where until they can get us on a flight to La Paz. One thing we know for sure is that Gwen isn't going to make it. Apparently, she's really sick with food poisoning. I wonder if it's just a ruse since she didn't want to go to this reunion anyway. Not going requires a solid excuse, complete with doctor's note, because, if not, you won't get your last scholarship payment at the end of the year. I had considered faking an illness but it's not worth it and, anyway, I want to have the complete Fulbright experience. Otherwise, I would feel like I'd fallen short.

Gwen not coming means there's automatically at least one seat available. Finally, they establish there's one more, so Zeke and I get on the plane at the last minute…and in first class! This is only the second time I've flown first class and, though there's not much in the way of extra amenities, it makes us feel special. Actually, I'm wrong, there *are* extra amenities in the way of limitless free drinks but, since I don't drink, I'm happy with sparkling water. Zeke polishes off three alcoholic beverages during the two hour flight though he doesn't seem worse-for-wear because of it. We have a rousing conversation the whole way there and, though he's clearly a bit of a party dude, he's also really nice, and smart (as you'd expect from a Fulbrighter).

Several of us share a shuttle van to the hotel. As we whiz through the main part of La Paz, I find myself in major culture shock. This town looks like any Southern Californian town, even though it's nearly at the farthest tip of Baja California. There are Walmarts and Targets and lots of traffic—about as far from my sweet little San Agustín as you can get. *Just let me get through this*, I think, *and home to where I belong.*

We have the first night in La Paz free so a group of us go out to a place for dinner that some of them, who've already been in town partying for a few days, recommend. Yeah. They're young. I feel like I'm at a college rave rather than an academic gathering.

We've been told that tomorrow, Tuesday, we're going on a boat trip to a nearby island called Espiritu Santo for a beach day, which originally had been scheduled for Thursday but, since the weather will be better for it tomorrow, they changed it. I'm somewhat horrified by this eventuality. My stomach is not in good shape and a day on a boat and then on a beach eating either ham sandwiches or ceviche for lunch, which is what appears to be on the menu, sounds dreadful. I'm sure there won't be a handy bathroom, and I absolutely cannot tolerate that much time in the sun. In the morning, I plan to tell the organizer I won't be going. It's an optional activity so I can't be penalized for it.

Oh, by the way, I paid extra to have a room to myself. This was not highly encouraged but I need the quiet and the privacy. I'm the only one who has it so I try not to make a big deal out of it. I'm just too ~~old~~ mature to be "roomies" with someone.

The space is nice, as I'd expect from this level of hotel: a beautiful king bed in a large room, with a desk, comfy arm chair, high ceilings, a ceiling fan, mini fridge, a private (sort of) deck with a view of the docks, and a modern bathroom *with* toilet seat. In fact, the first thing I do after I get back from the restaurant is take a shower. The water pressure is sheer and utter bliss.

At our house in San Agustín, we have miserable water pressure. It's barely more than a trickle and it takes a long time to get hot. Then, it's too hot, so you try to balance it with cold, then you play the too cold/too hot game for a while until you finally get it right, but you want to get out of there as quickly as possible anyway, because one small trickle of water of any temperature is not ideal.

I could live in the shower in this hotel room.

This morning, we have two hours of meetings before the group sets sail for Espiritu Santo. After the welcome, we get right into the presentations, seventy to get through in three days. They're starting with those who have prepared PowerPoint presentations, which is nearly everyone, and will be going in alphabetical order according to first name. Thank God, otherwise I'd be going almost last and I can't take that kind of agony. Since there are a lot of names that come before Georgina, they're not going to get to me today anyway.

The meeting wraps up around ten, and the gang heads off to the boat launch while I retire to my nice, quiet room. Though my stomach is still funky, I will need to eat so, at about 11:00 I wander up the beach to see if I can find a restaurant that looks decent. When

I say decent, I mean nice, but not too expensive. This area of La Paz is resort city—very touristy, although most of the restaurants are farther up the beach, which is actually a bay. La Paz is situated in the Gulf of California, and there are no waves at all in this little inlet. It's pretty, and the water is a beautiful turquoise blue, though a bit chilly this time of year for swimming, but not really my idea of a beach.

Finally, I see a hotel that has a sign for a restaurant and I go check it out. It's perfect. Kind of an indoor/outdoor café with sandwiches, salads, etc., and not too pricey. I seat myself at a table for two in the shade, and the waiter comes to greet me, relieved I speak Spanish because he was afraid he was going to have to deal with another English speaking tourist. I order two sandwiches: one for now and one for later because I'm going to need dinner. The sandwich is served on a wonderful whole-grain bread with a side of delicious refried beans and a salad. My other sandwich, packed up to go, comes with waffle fries, which will probably be soggy when I get to them later. I generally don't like eating alone in a restaurant, but I feel mysterious and exotic, sitting here by myself in this gorgeous place.

Back at the hotel, I take a nap and spend the rest of the afternoon getting caught up on some Netflix series Jon doesn't care about. This is the me-time I've needed though I didn't realize it.

Bright and early this morning, and by that I mean 8:00, we're back in the meeting room. Breakfast is served at seven but, in order to have more time to sleep in, I've brought my own homemade granola and small boxes of milk so I can have breakfast in my room.

The presentations are actually pretty interesting and even fun. It's great to learn about what everyone has been up to, and what they find particularly compelling in their area of Mexico. I'd expected them to focus more on community projects or teaching, but a lot of them are kind of like Instagram stories, complete with photos of all their friends, the food they've eaten, and places they've visited.

Damn, people have been traveling a lot more than Jon and I. We'll have to get on that.

They get to me shortly before lunch. I happen to be wearing my San Agustín T-shirt that I got for Christmas, and I immediately get a huge round of applause just for that. Bolstered, I launch into my presentation. As photos of my extraordinary women fill the screen behind me, I speak with passion about how strong they are, how talented, brilliant, and dedicated; how they are the movers and shakers of their communities, how they inspire everyone around them to be better, including me. By the time I'm done, I am almost in tears from the emotion that fills me in speaking of these women.

As my audience claps and wipes tears from their own eyes, I head back to my seat and, as I do, I hear someone say, "Nobody wants to go after Georgina." This gives me a moment of satisfaction. Not that it's a competition. Not at all. Yet…I do tend to be competitive when it comes to this kind of thing, and I can't help but feel a bit smug.

I'm not saying mine is the only excellent presentation because of course there are several, yet I do experience another jolt of pride when, at break time, one of the ETAs tells me the people at his table have voted my presentation the best so far.

Lunch is late in being served…like 2:00 which is very late for me and I'm about to eat my arm. This is the first meal I've had at the hotel and it is lackluster—lackluster and meager. Thank God I've got snacks with me—actually I have more snacks than there was lunch. There are more presentations after lunch, lasting until 6:00, and then another ho-hum meal. After that, many of the ETAs plan to party the night away but not me. I'm not about to go shake it at some disco with a bunch of twenty-somethings so I head to bed early.

Day three: Yet more presentations. It's exhausting. We finally get to the ones people haven't prepared a PowerPoint for. Oddly, these are some of the most compelling. One of the last people to go is a young woman who shares how she was accosted on the streets of her town. She escaped unharmed, but deeply shaken. The people she'd spoken to about it in the aftermath asked her questions about how she was dressed and why she was out by herself at night. In short, she didn't get any resolution to her feelings of fear and shame over the event. She's so brave to share this with us. When she finishes, she walks back to her table and I instinctively rise and go to her, wrapping her in an embrace. She sobs into my shoulder as the meeting continues, oblivious. In this moment I realize my maturity is more of an asset than I thought in this program. I'm able to act as a sympathetic and almost maternal figure to her, clearly something she's needed and hasn't gotten since the attack occurred.

After another extremely late and boring lunch, we finish the day with a few hours of interactive seminars, in which we explore issues like preconceived cultural assumptions and differences, and our strengths and weaknesses both as teachers and cultural ambassadors—interesting, but I'm so done sitting in meetings.

We're on our own for dinner tonight but, before we make any plans, some of us head over to a nearby beach, one that I haven't been to, to watch the sunset. I'm thinking, *maybe this is a real beach, with waves!* It's not, but the sunset is pretty. Everyone is vague about dinner plans and I'm too hungry to postpone eating any longer. There's nothing in the way of stores out on this neck of the peninsula but, as I'm walking back to the hotel, I spy a gas station with a market in it. How bad could it be? It turns out to be a little sketchy but they do have some food options including sandwiches that look like they might have been made today. I buy two, one for dinner and one for lunch tomorrow, plus nuts, chips, dip, and anything I can get ahold of that will sustain me for the night.

Today, we say good-bye to La Paz. No meetings, thank God. I partake of the hotel breakfast buffet which is a thousand times better than what they've been serving us for lunch because I don't have to meet the group that has agreed to share a transport van to the airport until 9:00.

We get there in plenty of time for the flight to Mexico City, which leaves at 11:30. As we wait, I chat with some Mexican/American ETAs whom I hadn't gotten a chance to get to know. They probably thought this white lady wasn't relevant to their experience in the world, but we end up making each other laugh and I feel accepted by them. On the plane, we go our separate ways. Once we land in Mexico City, I follow the directions that an ETA who lives in Pachuca gave me for the bus.

I find the bus terminal easily since it's practically inside the airport. I'm on the prowl for snacks for the road. Finding some chips and nuts, I'm soon nestled in a comfy, dare I say, luxurious seat on the nicest bus I've ever been on, complete with wi-fi and TV screens at each seat with a variety of entertainment options.

I while away the time chatting with my mom on the phone because she wants to know every detail of my time in La Paz, and this is a great time to catch her up. Before I know it, the two hours have flown by and we're already in Pachuca. As soon as I start to think that I'll be catching a cab and home to Jon in less than an hour, I realize it's a long way from the outskirts of Pachuca to the bus station, and takes another half hour to get there. Now, I'm starving and just want to be home. (I'm sorry/not-sorry; I have a high metabolism and need to eat at regular intervals as you might have guessed by now.) We've planned a dinner out at La Hacienda tonight to celebrate my homecoming but I can't hold out for that. I buy a tuna *paste* at the bus station, hoping it won't be blazing hot but, of course it is—so spicy I can hardly eat it and I have gotten used to very spicy food. Why does tuna need to be so spicy? I eat it anyway because it's all I've got, in the cab, hurtling, yet again, along the highway between Pachuca and San Agustín without a seatbelt. It's growing dark and I'm anxious to be home.

I finally arrive at about 6:30 and Jon and I head straight for La Hacienda, where I get a comforting and delicious bowl of spaghetti Bolognese (the only place in town to get such a continental dish). San Agustín is still San Agustín and I feel warm and welcomed to be back. I have the weekend to relax before school starts up on Monday. Cristina has assured me she's revived the writing workshop, so I'm looking forward to seeing how that goes.

1,850,000 Steps

Jon's dad has passed away. It was imminent since he was 97 years old, and had been on the decline but, still, it's very sad. He had been in the hospital for COVID of all things; we couldn't be sure he had had all his vaccines. Sure enough, he succumbed. He had been going downhill for a couple of years before that, under Jon's sister's care in California, and not entirely lucid as of late. Happily, about a week ago, as we were walking down the street in San Agustín, we got a call from him, which is unusual since we can barely get service in our own house much less on the street. Jon chatted with him whenever service was available, but I hadn't spoken to him in a while. Honestly, he'd been going in and out of remembering we were in Mexico (at one point he thought we were in Africa). During this conversation, we both got to tell him what an amazing time we were having, and how much we loved and missed him. That was the last time we spoke to him.

Jon has been ready to launch into action since we got the news, and I've been looking at plane tickets to Las Vegas, which is where his dad wanted to be buried, in a military cemetery next to his wife as they had lived in that city for many years. There are all kinds of delays, however, the first of which has to do with Jon's sister trying to decide whether to bury or cremate him. I don't mean to be callous, but the burial is like $10,000, and the cremation is $1000 so it seems to me there's no argument since he hadn't specified. But Jon's sister is being swayed by the director of the funeral home, who of course is voting for the former option. That, and we have to figure out from the V.A. when they can do military honors graveside, and a few other complicated things, one of which is getting the death certificate. All of these things are in Jon's sister's hands at the moment though he's trying to help, but she is not one used to making these kinds of plans and decisions.

And so, even though everyone in San Agustín is flooding Jon with their condolences (I posted on Facebook about it, and those who follow me here spread the news like wildfire), and expect him to be distraught and fly off to the U.S. any day now, he's actually handling it very calmly, and doesn't want to be make a big deal of it. Also, there's no point in him going until the remains can be transferred to Las Vegas and that doesn't appear to be happening any time soon. The body has been in refrigeration at the funeral home already for a week while these decisions are being made, which seems like a long time to me.

In fact, despite the Facebook post, we've kind of been trying to keep the news on the down-low, though I told Rico right away in case I was going to need time off to help Jon with the arrangements, etc. He's been very sympathetic. I don't know if I've mentioned it, but Rico and Jon hit it off from the start and he's very protective of Jon—more so than of me if you want to know the truth.

1,850,000 to 1,900,000 Steps

Before the death of Jon's dad occurred, we had been invited to Maya's birthday party in the mutual courtyard of our houses, and we intended to go regardless because, why not? They didn't know about Jon's dad's passing yet and we were not inclined to tell them because we didn't want to spoil the mood.

In hilarious fashion, they put Chula on the roof so she wouldn't get in the way and gobble up the food. They put up an awning and arranged a long table and chairs under it. Then, around 5:00, Claudio started up the grill and we wandered out to see how we could help. We contributed some beer and soda but, other than that, they didn't need our assistance. Jon kept Claudio company at the grill, taking turns with a partially melted blow-dryer, traditionally used to make the fire hot. Soon after, their friends and other family members arrived, and Claudio started serving up the grilled steak and various sausages, which we ate with fresh tortillas, guacamole, and salsa. I was thinking how delicious and cool the guacamole looked so I put a big scoop on my taco, only to find that it was literal fire in my mouth: jalapeños, of course. From then on I stayed away from it, but everything else was delicious. Claudio played music, everyone was having fun, and finally Miriam served the chocolate cake she'd made for the occasion, at which time everyone sang "*Las mañanitas*" to Maya. She shyly laughed and somewhat reluctantly gave into what is either a family or, possibly, a local tradition, of taking a big bite of the cake without using hands or utensils.

I kind of feel like this event brought us even closer to their family. In fact, they are becoming among our favorite people in San Agustín. Miriam and I rely on each other for a lot of neighborly things like opening the front gate for each other if there's a package or visitor, letting Maya in when she forgets her keys (or me when the same happens), helping each other out with water deliveries because God knows you don't want to miss the water delivery guy, or you'll be hauling huge bottles of filtered water all over town. We've even taken care of Chula for them when they couldn't get home in time to feed her or were out of town overnight.

They love Lupita, incidentally, having met her at our Thanksgiving party, and having often glimpsed her through our window when she has full-on, ears-laid-back, howling stand-offs with Chula through the glass. Lupita isn't at all scared of the fearsome-looking Akita. I have a feeling that all Chula wants to do is play and all Lupita wants to do is tear her head off.

In evidence of the growing friendship between our families, not long after Maya's birthday party, Miriam and Claudio invite us to go have *barbacoa* with them in Actopan. *Barbacoa* is something one can eat at any time of the day, but breakfast is a popular time for it. We go with them in their car at 10:00 in the morning on this particular Wednesday to this huge kind of food court in Actopan. This happens every Wednesday because that is the day of Actopan's *tianguis*, which is nothing like San Agustín's. The Actopan *tianguis* takes over the whole city and, on the outskirts, cars, livestock, and other large items are sold. This area is where the food court is so we drive right there, park in the dirt "parking lot," and enter this building where vendors have set up stands, each selling their own version of *barbacoa*, or tamales, or roasted chicken or whatever. Claudio and Miriam have their favorite stand, so we make our way to the back of the building and sit at picnic tables and benches. Claudio orders, and in minutes a lady arrives bearing a huge plate of meat, fresh tortillas, and salsa. The meat, of course, is the roasted sheep, with plenty of fat. Claudio dives right in, using his tortilla to snag the fattiest pieces, and then pours the salsa on. Jon and I proceed more cautiously, avoiding the excess of fat, and testing out the salsa before going crazy. I have to admit, it's all delicious, but seems like a very heavy meal for so early in the day. Afterwards, Claudio and Miriam gather up the leftovers, and we offer to pay, since they've driven us there and introduced us to this favorite ritual of theirs, which, apparently, they partake of nearly every Wednesday. There's a little push back, but not much, proving that Cristina's overreaction to my paying for our lunch in Tula was exactly that—an overreaction. Claudio and Miriam seem grateful to have us pay, and we're happy to do it. On the way out, Claudio buys a kind of candy called *palanqueta,* which is like nut brittle but not as hard, made with pecans or peanuts or both, and *piloncillo,* that natural, dried sugar cane juice. He tells me to try it and I fall in love with it. Now, I eat it every chance I get with no blood sugar crash. This is part of what I consider the magic of Mexico. As long as I avoid food poisoning, I can pretty much eat whatever I want with no ill effect.

1,900,000 to 1,990,000 Steps

(including bike rides)

We're still in limbo in regards to Jon going to Las Vegas. I'm not going to be able to go because it would mean missing a lot of school and it's expensive. Cremation has been decided upon, but not carried through yet because the funeral home is booked. What? How does that happen? How are bodies just lingering in refrigeration waiting their turn? It's now been three weeks since Jon's dad passed, in which the body spent ten days in the morgue and now another ten at the funeral home. This seems disrespectful to me and, frankly, pisses me off, but there's nothing we can do about it. In the meantime, Jon's sister is trying to get the death certificate to the V.A. who need it to set up the graveside honor guard, and then we'll have to see what date they give us for the internment. This is crazy.

We're trying to just get on with our lives in the meantime and February is turning out to be a busy month. Cristina has stayed true to her word and has reorganized the writing workshop by basically making it mandatory that her chemistry students attend. This is not exactly the scenario I had in mind but I'll take it. Attendance will be taken and those who complete the ten week "course," as she's calling it, will receive a certificate. (Based on the fact that my collection of certificates is always growing, I've come to realize they are a big deal here.) The administration has made up a flyer for my workshop, and it remains open to anyone, at UPFIM or not, who wants to participate. We had our first meeting just a couple of days ago, and it was full of young, bright faces, enthusiastic for the opportunity to put pen to paper and express the things that have been on their minds. Cristina and I came up with a new curriculum for the workshop, which is that the first ten minutes is spent reviewing Spanish grammar (they may be university kids but, trust me, they need it), then twenty minutes working on their projects individually. Then, we have ten minutes in which I review anyone's work who wants me to look at it, and in which they can share what they've written with a partner. Finally, we spend five minutes of writing spontaneously from a prompt I provide, and the last five or ten minutes sharing what we wrote with the class. The projects they've chosen span quite a variety of genres. Some are writing diaries and memoirs, some short stories, some poetry; one of them is working on a novel, another is writing letters to the father that abandoned him, and another is writing about music, which is his passion. I'm glad we decided to let men participate. They are some of the most dedicated writers.

Agcv = More input from Lupita on the keyboard. Translation: I'm hungry, feed me.

Today is Valentine's Day, which is a major event here. In the morning, the teachers gather for a catered party, consisting of enchiladas, with a choice of chicken, *arrachera* which is thinly sliced beef, or an egg on top, and either green or red sauce, or both (called *divorciadas*). Another option is *chilaquiles*, with the choice of sauces and meats. The WhatsApp chat thread on this topic, started by Lina, who was in charge of the ordering, was hilarious, with Lina trying to get everyone to decide on what they wanted, and to do it in time to place the order. It was like herding cats.

She finally managed to organize it all and, this morning, the restaurant delivers it with coffee, freshly squeezed orange juice, and fruit—all about an hour late, though no one seems too concerned about getting to class. For this event, the teachers have decided to exchange gifts in a Secret Santa sort of way. Yet, all the teachers agreed that the gift had to be an organizer case for markers and such. There was even talk on the thread about where to purchase them and how much they were. This kind of ruins any element of surprise, I think, but so be it. I drew Antonia as my secret Valentine. I looked all over San Agustín for the organizer, but couldn't find it. Finally, I asked Irene, Antonia's best friend, where I could find one, and she said Walmart—which is either in Progreso or Pachuca. The party is only a couple of days away, and I don't have time to go to either town to hunt the thing down. Irene says she has to get one for her Valentine anyway, so she'll get one for Antonia and I can pay her back. At the party, when we exchange the gifts, everyone ends up with an identical organizer except for me. Adela, the actress, chose me as her secret Valentine, and got me an organizer with pink ponies and sparkles all over it because that's basically her style.

As for the students, they've decorated the doors of their classrooms in Valentine themes, and the winner gets a pizza party. In the classes I'm teaching today (when we actually get to them), and that I've taught over the last few days, our activity has been for each student to write a love letter, in English, to someone special in their lives—a friend or girl/boyfriend, for example—and decorate them. I choose the winner, and that person puts their letter in a special mailbox, which Adela has named "Love on the Brain." The love note will be delivered today by a person designated as cupid. Wow, some of these students are true poets. I wish I could get them in my writing workshop.

After those enchiladas for breakfast, though, I'm feeling kind of off. When I'm done with classes for the day, I go on home, thinking no one needs me anymore. As I pass Cafée Rinkon, I see that one of Marco's little girls is there hanging out with her grandpa, so I give her my pink, sparkly organizer.

At home, I've just laid down for a nap when Rico texts me, wanting me back at the school to help with the afternoon's party for the students. I slog back to hang out in the heat while a few couples dance to loud Cumbia music and we eat cold pizza. I end up playing

Uno with one young man who is intellectually challenged—a sweet kid I've had in some of my classes. I think it makes him feel included in a day that he otherwise wouldn't get to participate in much and so I feel I've earned my Valentine's Day merit badge.

Jon and I have recently started taking classes in hñähñu. Arlo (naturally) has organized this course which takes place twice a week at 5:00 in the evening. It's a little late in the day for me as by that time I'm pretty much just wanting to get home and eat, but I'm very interested in learning about this part of the culture of the Valle del Mezquital. I've decided one day a week is enough since this class really is geared toward the people here who are connected to the indigenous bloodline and who want to learn the language of their ancestors—some not so very distant, or even still living. It's a hard language to learn, that's for sure, because it's not connected at all to Spanish, except that there are a few Spanish words thrown in when the one you need doesn't exist in hñähñu. (Please note that I spell this word without capitalization because that's how it's written. Also, you see that it does share some of the alphabet with Spanish. It does not have a unique alphabet.)

I truly do love being in a classroom learning any language, even though I'm a bit frustrated that the words are so hard to remember and pronounce. However, my difficulty with it is nothing compared to Jon's, who not only is not particularly adept at languages, but has to sit through a class learning one foreign language, hñähñu, taught in another, Spanish, which is still hard for him to grasp. In other words, the teacher, a lovely man named Patricio who speaks hñähñu fluently and whom we call *xänäthe* (shawn-ah-teh), the word for teacher in that language, gives all his explanations in Spanish. He speaks no English at all. I admire Jon for trying and he attends the classes with great dedication.

From Jon: here's the deal, I took meticulous notes during my time in this class and, in the beginning, I was generally able to keep up because the teacher would write a phrase on the board in *hñähñu* and beneath that he would translate that phrase into Spanish. I, in turn, would quickly translate that Spanish to English on my phone, and on and on.... A small problem, however, emerged a few weeks in when the xänäthe *would write the phrase in hñähñu and proceed to talk about it in Spanish. From that point forward I continued to take notes as such, interspersing them with internal commentary that at least amused me while awaiting the completion of that evening's entertainment. What follows here are some of those comments:*

....nujhu d'i petzhu 'na ra fani Uds - nujhu gui petzhu 'na ra fani

> Today I am in a class listening to sounds of a language - without even a translation into Spanish. A perfect description of being - "in-over-my-head" 😵 ....Ya bede de n'a hasta nàte

> ... dada – papa, da-dá – sir, nana – mama, na-ná – ma'am.

> The teacher speaks Spanish and explains in Spanish. I, on the other hand, speak English pretty well. Wow! I once attempted to learn Italian. The teacher there at least provided explanations in English. Still to be fair, that didn't go well either. 😊 ....zi doni husa do gätzi di gätzi

---

My last day of class:
...ya ga ma - me voy, ya maga ma - ya me voy, ya da m'o

> Here we are again, xänäthe *is quizzing the class on what we have already learned. Nothing is being written on the board in any language. Can we say, "lost?" Not yet, and possibly never. That word has not yet been provided, despite that*

it perfectly describes my status here. He speaks the word in hñähñu expecting us to translate into Spanish 😟😃😝😵 ❓ *to be fair, he kindly provides the explanation - also in Spanish.*

Now he's singing a song. OMG!!!! 🔇 *Hello? Hello? Hello? Hello? Hello? He just wrote the words of the song on the board: nxungärida gra póxuini nxungärida grä c'ajuihni antes drä bathori ñana ge antes drä b'atha ma dädä gäl*

Nice!

I do appreciate that Georgina is now helpfully playing a recording of the song. Everyone happily sings along. I'm not joining in, but no one notices. Georgina just sent me a copy of the recording in WhatsApp. Cool! I'm sure I'll be playing it in the car on a regular basis. I do notice the words being sung don't seem to actually relate to the words (such as they are) on the board. Oh my! Georgina asks intelligent questions to get clarification. And receives answers accordingly. Sigh....

Ga nzenjua thui, hasta luego - nos saludamos pronto, ya ga ma

One other, completely unrelated, bit of interest is that Jon and I purchased a couple of bicycles not long ago. They are "beater bikes" as Jon says: old, used, and without certain features like kickstands or gears, but they are a good way to go exploring to the farther reaches of the town and beyond. We've really been enjoying taking the bikes out in the late afternoon, once the day has cooled off a bit, riding out past fields and farms. I love the feeling of the wind in my hair (because helmets are hard to come by here) as we take in the beauty of the green pastures and the blue-grey hills in the distance. Sometimes, when I'm riding along, I think to myself, "This is Mexico." That's all. Not, this is Mexico for good or bad, just that

I'm here, loving it for everything it is and is not. This has become my place.

Additionally, the bikes have made picking up and dropping off the laundry a lot easier. On one of our excursions exploring the town, we discovered a small laundry place that is not as far as the one on the outskirts though not close enough to walk without putting the stuff in the rolling suitcase. This place is reliable, they do a great job, and it's reasonably priced. Jon has taken to strapping the laundry bag to the handlebars of his bike, and he takes it himself—there and back in ten minutes. Finally, we have figured out how to get laundry done in this town without a huge hassle.

1,990,000 to 2,180,000 Steps

At last, the date has been set for Jon's dad's memorial service and internment of ashes with the military honor guard at graveside: March 25. More than a month away still. This is because the soldiers who do the honors are booked until then. Apparently, a lot of World War II and Korean War veterans are passing away at the moment as they are all in their 90s now or older. But at least the body has been cremated and Jon's sister has the remains in her possession. Of course, there was a big to-do about what kind of urn to get but we left that up to her. Now, we can make plane and hotel reservations for Jon's trip. This is all kind of tricky, though, because we have reservations to fly to Oaxaca (pronounced Wah-HAH-kah) on April 1st. We plan to stay just three days because that's as long as we're comfortable leaving Lupita, who will be in the care of the neighbors. Between now and then we also have a trip planned with Rico to another magical town, and a weekend in Veracruz with Cristina. All these things have been carefully planned out not to interfere with two other things: Anna's baby's baptism on March 4th, which she invited us to not long after we met, and a truly exciting thing that happens this very day, the arrival of my dear friend Teresa.

Teresa and I have been friends for just over twenty years when we were teaching English together in New York. What really cemented it was that we were both in the school building on the morning of 9/11. I'm not going to go into that whole thing, as it's still traumatizing to think about and not the purpose of this story, but suffice it to say we fled Manhattan together that morning, on foot and by bus, across the river to where we both lived in Queens, relying on each other to get us through that terrifying ordeal. We have been fast friends ever since, and Teresa, an intrepid traveler, is making her way by bus to us today from Mexico City, where she's spent a few days seeing the sights.

She'll arrive about 3:00, but I have to teach until 5:00 so Jon is meeting her at the bus and bringing her to the school so she can see it.

I'm waiting for them in the English office when I hear their voices outside, and run to greet her. What a wonderful sight it is to see my friend, here in this place, when it's been about four years since I saw her last.

I wanted her to meet Rico but he's gone for the day, so we head over to hñähñu class as I thought it would be fun for her to experience. Poor thing is pretty tired though, so we cut out early (*From Jon: Thank you, God!*) and walk to Los Volcanes, asking Arlo to meet us there for tacos. He gets there via car about the time we arrive on foot, and we enjoy a dinner of *tacos al pastor*. The two of them hit it off famously, as I knew they would. Teresa speaks Spanish very well and so we get to have a fun bilingual conversation with Jon keeping up the best he can.

After that, we walk home and star gaze at the alignment of Jupiter and Mars with the moon, a meaningful portent for this visit. Teresa is immediately struck by the charm of San Agustín. She gets it one hundred percent in the same way we do and that makes me extremely gratified.

At home, we exchange some gifts: a welcome-bag of San Agustín goodies from us to her, and, from her to us organic chocolate and cookies, plus my favorite hair dye. She went to the trouble to send us similar treats for my birthday, a very thoughtful thing to do as it's extremely hard to send packages from the U.S. to here. She also sent a birthday card separately that only just got to me, three months late, a bit soggy, but still readable. That's the kind of thing she does—always thinking about others.

This morning we get right on to an adventure we've been planning for weeks. At 9:00 AM, we're on the combi to Progreso, ultimately heading to Las Grutas de Tolantongo, a sort-of hot springs resort, deep in the hills of Hidalgo, where a hot water river provides pools and caves for bathing. Apparently, it's only one of two places like it in the world; the other is in South Korea.

We have no idea how to change busses in Progreso to get the one we need to Ixmiquilpan (Eex-mee-KEEL-pahn), from whence we will catch another to Las Grutas (meaning the grottos, or caves). But, naturally, there is a kind lady on the combi who tells us to get off where she does, and to follow her to the bus stop because she, too, is going to Ixmiquilpan. We do, and she walks with us the two or so blocks to where we get on the next bus with her. She assures us she will tell us where to get off to get the bus to Las Grutas because she's getting off there too.

The ride to Ixmiquilpan is sort of grueling because it's fraught with speed bumps all along the way—one after another—abrupt and jarring. The landscape is desert-y, scattered with small, unremarkable towns. After about an hour, we finally arrive and, at this point, we've sort of had it with busses, and are considering taking a cab the rest of the way. We let our guide know this, and she immediately begins approaching the taxis that are lined up near the bus stop, bargaining with the drivers to find us the best deal. She gets us a ride for about 30 bucks, which is perfect. We thank our angel, as we've come to think of her, profusely. Teresa wants to offer her something for her kindness but I suggest she doesn't. This is how people are in this region: generous and helpful just for the sake of it.

The cab driver is friendly and talkative. I'm sitting in the front seat and he's telling me all about the area, and information about Las Grutas. We drive through hilly, arid land, until we start to ascend in earnest. Up and up we go to the summit of the road, and then we begin to descend into a canyon amidst high, rocky hills—almost mountains but not quite. Here, the scenery is spectacular though still quite desert-like. The road provides vistas that look out over miles and miles of dramatic, rocky terrain. We go down one hair-pin turn after another which the driver navigates skillfully. I'm grateful for this, and also glad I sat in the front seat because I tend to get car sick on this kind of road. Finally, we see, at the bottom of the canyon, a slash of pale, turquoise blue, something that looks out of place in this desert and also surreal because I've never seen water that color. We continue to descend, past a hotel, and a series of pools built into the hillside of the same color blue. At last, we reach the bottom and the resort. When I say resort, I'm being very generous because it's all pretty rustic, even that hotel we passed on the way. Here, at the entrance to the park, let's call it, where you pay 180 pesos per person (about $9.00), there is another, smaller, more rustic-looking hotel, a cantina, and a shop selling all kinds of necessities and souvenirs.

After we pay to enter, Jon and I buy towels for 100 pesos each since we didn't bring any, plus water shoes, which is recommended. We then proceed to the changing rooms where I don my total coverage swim suit—kind of like a wetsuit, but lighter. I'm not about to expose my skin to the blazing sun. Even though it's February, it's quite warm out and the sun is just as intense as it is everywhere else in the Valle del Mezquital. The next stop before entering the main cave is an outdoor locker area for storing our stuff. We optimistically store everything there but hats, towels, phones, and sunglasses, which meets with approval by the guards at the entrance to the stairs leading to the cave. Nothing else is allowed past that point other than your bathing suit and water shoes.

We bound up the steep stairs, only to be told that, before we enter the cave, we have to leave our phones, hats, and towels on a nearby fence for fear of them being swept off into the strong current. Some people have come supplied with clear phone cases which they sold in the shop, and which you can hang around your neck for taking photos, but we weren't aware we'd need them. Anyway, everyone else is leaving their stuff at the fence so we do too, and then we wade into a beautifully warm stream, under a cool waterfall, and into the cave. The cave is huge, with a vaulted ceiling gushing warm water. Since this is part of where the river flows through, there's a strong current, but there's a net fence keeping you from careening down a waterfall into the lower section. There are quite a few other people in the cave, but it's still an amazing experience, swimming around in that body-temperature water, with steam and a resounding echo swirling around you. It's interesting to us that, in spite of Hidalgo generally not being that much of a tourist destination, this place, in particular, has attracted people from all over the world— from Demark to Australia, from Japan to Greece. They have all found this particular spot in the middle of literally nowhere. The place is amazing and everyone who has bothered to make the journey knows it. We all feel we have found something extraordinary and even magical, in the remote hills of Mexico.

After that, we check out what is referred to as the "tunnel," but it's narrow and dark and we can't see the exit on the other side so we decide that's a no. After another soak in the cave, we head back down the steps and then down a long path to that pale blue river. We've chosen a good day to come because, overall, it's not terribly crowded. The river is divided into large sections, perhaps fifty to seventy feet square, via small dams, creating pools while allowing water to continue flowing downstream. We find a section with hardly anyone in it and immerse ourselves in the purely blissful warm water. It's not quite as hot as a jacuzzi, which is fine with me. In fact, it's perfect: the kind of warmth you could soak in forever and never chill off. Soon, the other people who were inhabiting our section of the river leave and we have this expansive pool all to ourselves. I find a spot in the shade, out of the current. Teresa goes to bask against a rock like a mermaid. Jon positions himself where the water pounds against him like a massage. Each in our own worlds, we are in ecstasy. The water has a softness to it, caused, I imagine, by whatever minerals make it that opaque blue. It feels good to immerse myself and take in the health benefits, which is one reason people come to this place.

There are other areas of the park to explore. One is called La Gloria, an area which requires paying another admission to enter. We've been told it's the best part but we don't really want to pay another entrance fee and, besides, we're so happy in the river. Another option is those man-made pools we saw on the way in, but that would require getting on a combi for a fifteen-minute ride and we just don't feel like it. Nothing could be better than this.

After a while, we decide it's time to eat since it's going on 2:00. Also, we realize we have a good two-hour ride home so better not to dally too long. There aren't really any taxis from here either. The available combis that go to Ixmiquilpan leave on set schedules, the next one being 3:30. There's only one after that, at 5:30. So we get our clothes from the lockers and change in the changing rooms, then meet at the cantina for a lunch of grilled sandwiches and juice.

After that, we just relax until the combi leaves. I'm exhausted, having not slept well last night, but I'm also contented. My skin and hair feel soft and nourished from the water. I try to doze on the combi, but the hair pin turns and the speed bumps make it difficult. Finally, we get to Ixmiquilpan, and opt for a taxi from there. It's a much quicker and more comfortable ride back to San Agustín than the way we came.

At home, we shower and change. We grab a light dinner at a café we've never tried before for salads and crepes, which are decent, but not great.

Yesterday was a day to rest and chill in San Agustín. We took Teresa out around town, then she explored on her own for a while, and then we made dinner at home.

Today, we're off to Tula again. This time, we take the bus, which goes right there. It's a more economical option than a taxi, but it's kind of a pain because it's technically a commuter bus, and it quickly fills up with people, some of whom have to stand in the aisles. Plus, it makes a lot of stops, turning the forty-five-minute ride into more like an hour and fifteen. We're full of energy today so we don't care. Thankfully, there is no clown.

We zip along the path from the entrance, past the three corridors of *tchotchkes*, to the site. Teresa is appropriately awed by the sight of the warriors on the pyramid, and we are too because it just never gets old. Today we can take our time. We share with Teresa our knowledge of the history. When we get to the part about how the structures were originally covered in precious stones, Teresa and I, in our inevitably silly way, can't help joking about how the Toltecs must have been the first "bedazzlers." Though perhaps a bit irreverent, being in this place with her brings out the humor in all three of us, and we laugh our way through the site while still being properly wowed by the profundity of it. Teresa and Jon have no problem scampering to the top of the pyramid, but my knees are feeling iffy so I skip it. One time is plenty.

When we've taken everything in, and tromped all over the area, we head back to the entrance, trying to decide how we're going to get home. Jon and I have learned by now that there's always a way, even if it doesn't seem apparent. Certainly, we can wait for the bus but I'd rather not. We ask the guy at the ticket booth if he can call us a cab and he does. He asks where we're going and we tell him San Agustín. Like everyone else upon hearing that name, he doesn't seem too sure of it as a destination, but he manages to get us a cab, which scoops us up in the parking lot about 15 minutes later.

The driver seems pretty secure about where he's going but, once we hit Mixquiahuala, he veers off in a strange direction and eventually stops in some rural nook, announcing to us that we're there. Um, no, I say, we're not. Doubling down, he insists that it is, indeed, the place. It really doesn't take much to discover that he actually has no idea where San Agustín is, nor does his GPS. I tell him to head toward Progreso and that San Agustín is about 15 minutes beyond that. After several twists and turns, we're finally on the right path, and he manages to deliver us to our door. At that point, he quotes an extra 100 pesos onto the price originally agreed upon since he got lost and it took him more time to get us to where we were going. I object, stating that I gave him the correct directions and it's not our fault he got lost. I mean, isn't is a cab driver's job to know where to go? There's no point arguing with him, so I pay him the extra hundred, which I probably would have given him as a tip anyway.

We eat a light lunch at home and relax for the rest of the afternoon. Tonight, we're off to La Hacienda for dinner. Since we didn't get a chance to celebrate Teresa's birthday, which is the day before mine, dinner out at the nicest restaurant in San Agustín is on us—a celebratory birthday meal.

She loves the place, as everyone does, and we order drinks, appetizers, steaks, and dessert, while being honored for part of the meal by the presence of the owner, José, who seems quite taken with Teresa. We were kind of hoping this would be the case because, even though he says he has a girlfriend, it seems like that's not a very permanent arrangement. Since Teresa is single, and they're about the same age, we thought they might hit it off.

They seem to, and I start thinking about how to subtly pass him her number. You can't be too forward with these old school Mexican guys. At any rate, Teresa leaves tomorrow, so they won't see each other again, at least during this visit.

I'm sad because we've had such a good time having her here yet we've got more adventures coming right around the corner.

2,180,000 to 2,270,000 Steps

On this last day of February, I'm giving a Black History Month presentation at the school. This one is close to my heart. This one I've poured my soul into. Rico had sort of suggested that I do a Valentine's Day presentation, but that just seemed lackluster to me. Anyway, as we've seen, it's not that different in Mexico than in the U.S. No, if I was going to focus on U.S. culture, there's no better way to do that than to talk about Black history because, in my mind, there is no separation between American history and Black history—it's one and the same. Nor is there American culture without Black culture. In fact, I believe that Black culture is American culture, and vice versa. You might argue that various ethnic groups, including those that came from Europe like the Irish or the Germans, definitely the Italians, have a strong, individual culture in the U.S. You can even say that we are a melting pot in which all these cultures, as well as Asian, Latino, Middle Eastern, etc., come together. But if you look at American music, sports, fashion, film, art, literature, pop culture, politics, science, etc., none of those things would exist in any meaningful way without the African American contributions.

I've included all these cultural aspects in my presentation, highlighting as many great African American contributors in each category as I can. However, with limited time, I can only talk about so many. Besides, I'm also focusing strongly on the history of slavery in the U.S., and Civil Rights as well. If I'd had the chance in January to give a presentation on Dr. Martin Luther King Jr., on the day dedicated to him, I would have, but I am only given space to do four formal presentations at UPFIM during my time here. On MLK day, I gave an informal talk to the students in the classes I had, and was surprised to learn how much they knew about him, about the Civil Rights Movement, and especially about the problem of racism in the U.S. Sadly, a good portion of that racism has been directed at Mexicans and they know it.

I spent some time, as I was preparing my presentation over the last few weeks, comparing notes with the Peace Corps volunteer, Alexxa, who is currently placed on one of the campuses in UPFIM's network, about two hours away. We met on a couple of occasions and hit it off.

We decided to not exactly collaborate, but to share our presentations with each other as they evolved. She actually is African American, and is planning to focus heavily on the Black Lives Matter movement, including showing the video of George Floyd's murder. I'm ending my presentation with slides that explain the movement, illustrating the number of people of color who were murdered by police in just the past year by rolling slides of all those names (somewhere around 250), while playing Beyonce's "Hero." Honestly, I could hardly get through that part without tearing up when I practiced it at home.

When I get to the auditorium today, and get set up with Rico's help, prepared with the playlist I have for the music part—everything from ragtime to jazz to blues to rock to rap to the pop of today—I'm ready to speak calmly yet passionately on all aspects of the presentation. And when it comes to the end, to the role of names, I don't even speak. I just let the overwhelming number speak for itself. Afterwards, the students have great questions about injustice and racism, and I answer them in as straightforward a manner as I can.

With my major presentation now in the rear-view mirror, this weekend, I'm focusing on the event of the season: Anna's baby's baptism.

A bit dressed up, we head to the church on this Saturday morning—THE church—you'll notice I said, as there is only one, and it's the main one, in the *centro* of San Agustín, for the actual ceremony. This is a situation in which several babies are baptized from various families at once. It's a complete mass, including a sermon. Jon is great for sort of putting up with this since 1) he is not religious and does not like sitting in church and 2) he understands nothing of what is said. Yet, the sermon is quite nice and a little surprising, in that the priest talks about how one does not have to be baptized to be loved by God, be a child of God, and to enter into heaven. I don't think this is quite the usual Catholic point of view, but I don't really know that much about it either.

Unfortunately, Anna's baby isn't feeling well, so they sort of whisk him in for the part of the service where they apply the water and ask the vows of the parents, godparents etc., and then whisk him out again. This makes me concerned for the party later, but they're not going to cancel an event they've been planning for months and that will have at least 300 guests in attendance.

Around 3:00, we take a taxi to the small town of Bocamiño, just about ten minutes from San Agustín, to where the event is taking place. When we get there, we find a tent the size of a warehouse set up, very much like that baptism we went to with Arlo, and tables arranged inside. Anna's mom is there to greet us, she leads us to a table where a family is already seated, and introduces us. These congenial people are our group for the evening. The mom, a lady around my age wearing a ton of make-up and a rather flashy outfit is extremely gregarious and I enjoy talking to her. Her husband, on the other side of Jon, is quite dour, and her grown kids are nice but not that interested in us.

The hosts of the occasion have supplied huge amounts of food, as is always the case at these kinds of events, and we are happy to partake: the chicken *mole* with rice, the *carnitas* tacos and then the *barbacoa*, plus various appetizers in between. We're actually stuffed by the time the *barbacoa* arrives, but it would be rude not to inhale at least a couple of tacos.

Anna and her husband come around to greet us but the baby is ensconced elsewhere nearby, poor thing, apparently with some kind of respiratory ailment, being cared for in turn by Anna, her husband, her mom, and her sister. After the food, the band starts up, and my new friend and her husband leap up to dance. This is what they've been waiting for. They are practically pros, she's informed me, and that does seem to be the case as they burn up the dance floor. I'm a little nervous about trying out our swing moves but, since we impressed the crowd at the school Christmas party, I'm a little more inclined now. Besides, this time, as opposed to at the baptism Arlo took us to, we're dressed for it.

We take to the dance floor and everyone is pretty wowed, which gratifies me. Trust me, if you were to compare us to people who really dance swing well, you would not be impressed but, without that comparison, we hold our own.

At a break in the dancing, we are urged to take part in a rather strange ritual, which is that of the parents of the baby throwing coins into the midst of the guests crowded onto the dance floor, while everyone, old and young, dives for them. This is a crazy, and almost dangerous event, as the people show no mercy in grabbing for the money any which way they can. We let them have at it, and only end up with a few coins ourselves. Our lives aren't worth it.

After that, the cake is served, then the band starts up again and Anna, who has a beautiful voice, joins in with them. At this point they bring around bottles of booze—mostly tequila, which you're welcome to either imbibe on the spot or take home. We pass. We're not the most dedicated partiers in the world as you may have surmised by now. Case in point: at about 9:00, we decide we'd better be going as we're not sure how we're going to find a cab home. Anna's husband, a delightful person, walks us out to the road and waits with us as I send a text to the same cabbie who drove us there. He shows up in about ten minutes, during which time Anna's husband tells us that, as exhausted as they all are, they probably won't wrap up the party until about 3:00 AM. That's a twelve hour party, folks, and it's probably going to get wild, but we have no intention of sticking around to find out. We've had a great evening, but now it's time for bed.

It's been a week since the baptism, and today we're off to the Magical Town of Huasca de Ocampo with Rico and his family. Jon and I have booked a hotel there just for the night, our first overnight away from San Agustín together. We get the bus at 9:00, and meet Rico, his wife, and their ten-year-old son at the first bus stop in Pachuca a little after 10:00. This is only the second time I've met his wife, an English teacher whom I fall right into conversation with, in both of our languages, in the back seat of Rico's car. Jon sits in front with Rico so they can chat. Rico, by the way, is really into heavy metal rock of the 90s. As a result, we are serenaded by the likes of Fall Out Boy and Nirvana during the hour long drive to Huasca.

This town is in the mountains above Pachuca, where it's piney, though not quite green at this time of year since it's the dry season. It's also a place known for the legend of the gnomes who hide in the surrounding forests and in the cemetery, according to the guy who tiled our kitchen, who claimed to have seen one himself. As we drive into the main part of the town, that is the first thing that catches our eyes: gnome figurines being sold everywhere, and gnome themes on many shop and hotel names. We find a place to park, and wander into the main part of the downtown, where we see people waiting to snap a photo with a guy in a gnome suit for a few pesos. We have to get one—it's almost obligatory. Yet, aside from the kind of Disneylandish gnome presence, the town is beautiful, with stone buildings from centuries before, lots of cute cafes, and stalls selling all kinds of knickknacks and treats. The first thing we do is grab a table in the central marketplace, THE place for authentic, inexpensive food, Rico says. We have a wonderful meal and, after wandering the town a bit more, get back in the car and head to an "ecological park," as they call it, meaning, basically an outdoor recreation area, to see what's known as the Prismas Balsaticos, prism-shaped rock formations from which waterfalls tumble. Though I've seen photos of the place, nothing prepares me for how genuinely amazing it is.

The park is huge, with restaurants and shops, and filled with sight-seers, yet also spacious enough not to feel crowded. After we pay admission and park, we walk along trails and cross over a deep chasm on a suspension bridge, from where we can see the many waterfalls that emerge from somewhere underground and plunge into the river below. It's great to be out in the sunshine (though I have my umbrella) with Rico and his family in this relaxed atmosphere because he tends to be rather formal in his role at UPFIM. Even though I make it my goal to get him to laugh on a regular basis, a difficult but satisfying endeavor, he remains a bit buttoned up and serious in general. Today, though, he's completely chilled out, romping and having fun with his son, who's a great kid, smart as a whip.

We continue along the river until the path descends, down, down, down, to a stone plaza-type of area, where you can view one of the larger waterfalls from below, and even walk under it if you choose. This is where most of the visitors gather, enjoying the water and the spectacle of those incredible formations.

From Jon: Okay, I don't keep it all that much of a secret that I have a vivid imagination and, truthfully, this place simply couldn't have lived up to what I had imagined. When I heard the name of this place translated to Prisms I was totally looking forward to giant, well, prisms—with sunlight shining through them, refracting into wonderous rainbows radiating throughout a water-filled valley of stones. They were not quite that. Sure, I did see rainbows. I saw them occasionally appear in sprays of water that filled the air around the numerous roaring waterfalls cascading from the tops of, to be fair, huge prism shaped blocks of stone. Fortunately for me, I also happen to love rocks in general and have a large collection of my own, so while I did admire and appreciate what we were seeing, I couldn't help but feel that, although I'd been expecting magic at a Harry Potter level, I had no choice but to settle for magic that was a bit more down to earth, so to speak. All that said, the place was indeed quite spectacular in its own geologically awe-inspiring way. I was far from disappointed, but I did have to smack my imagination into its home, where it lives, ever-hopeful, in the back of my mind.

I eventually wander off to find a bathroom, and then we all head back up the path to some of the shops where Jon and I find a hand-painted dress for my kid's partner. When we've done and seen all, we pile back in the car and return to Huasca. I'm pretty worn out now because, in my typical manner, I didn't sleep well the night before in anticipation of this trip, so Jon and I go check into the hotel and take a brief nap. After that, we're hungry again, and we meet Rico and his family for another meal in the marketplace. They then head off, back to Pachuca, but we wander around the town some more and get Jon a margarita at one of the cafés.

After a slightly less than comfortable night in the hotel, we eat a delicious breakfast of enchiladas and eggs at one of the cafes, and then catch a combi to Pachuca, where we grab a cab back to San Agustín. This has been Lupita's first night in Mexico without us. Though she's been fed and looked after by Miriam and Maya, she's very happy to see us return. I'm sure she was nervous we would abandon her in this foreign place though I'm also pretty sure she's coming to think of it as home.

2,270,000 to 2,300,000 Steps

We are off to the coast of Veracruz today to spend the weekend in a town called Tecolutla with Cristina and her twelve-year-old son. I've been promising Jon a beach weekend, since he missed out on La Paz, and I'm hoping he'll get his fix, though the weather forecast for the coast isn't great. Cristina picks us up at about 11:00 in her comfortable SUV, her twelve-year-old son in the front serving as navigator. He seems pretty shy but Jon, Cristina, and I make up for it in conversation.

The hills of the Valle del Mezquital fade into the rearview mirror once we're well past Actopan. Once beyond Pachuca, the landscape becomes mountainous. We traverse it via tunnel after tunnel and, each time we emerge, a greater vista is revealed. I didn't know this kind of landscape existed in Hidalgo but now I see how magnificent the state really is. Vast mountainsides of evergreen forests rise in the distance for miles and miles, continuing through a portion of the state of Puebla, and into Veracruz.

As we come down out of the mountains, I let Cristina know I could use a bathroom. She pulls over at a rest stop and, as soon as we open the car doors, I know we're near the coast. A mild, humid breeze overtakes us. There's no mistaking that beach air. Yet we still have a way to go until we reach Tecolutla. Now, the scenery becomes tropical: lush greenery, palms, and twisting vines. We pass the Magical Town of Papantla, and the vegetation becomes even more dense. I'm thrilled to be seeing this aspect of Mexico. I've spent a fair amount of time on the west coast of the country, and have also been further north of Veracruz, to the state of Tamaulipas, which is on the east coast, but very industrial and more desert-y. On the west coast, and south, into Sinaloa and beyond, it's quite tropical. I know it well because Jon and I honeymooned in Mazatlán and, when I was a kid, I spent a week in Acapulco. Now, we couldn't go to Sinaloa if we wanted to, nor to certain other states such as Michoacan, which almost neighbors Hidalgo to the west (except that Mexico City gets in the way), or Guerrero, which is where Acapulco is located. These states and four or five others are on the U.S. State Department's list of those forbidden to people traveling on State Department business, which Fulbright scholars are, because of the danger of kidnapping. Sheesh. We've felt so safe in Hidalgo. It is, in fact, one of the safest states in Mexico and apparently Veracruz is too. Never-the-less, whenever we leave our state for any reason, we must notify COMEXUS. They are the ones responsible for our safety.

We finally come across a small but busy town I think must be Tecolutla, but not yet. We continue on along a wide river which Cristina says floods during the rainy season, to the extent that homes along the riverbank, and even the town, are often inundated. I guess the people just dry out and get on with their lives afterwards.

After another twenty minutes driving, we reach Tecolutla, kind of an unremarkable looking place, crowded with traffic. And, by the way, it's raining. We get to the hotel and check in, praying the weather will clear. The lady at the front desk informs us it likely will not. We're all hungry, so a few minutes later we meet downstairs to seek out a restaurant. I'm excited to have seafood since we're on the coast, and I noticed a couple of restaurants along the main road that mentioned trout in their names (after all, the river). We head for one of those and settle in. I don't see trout on the menu, just *pescado* (fish) so I ask if it's trout and the waiter says no, it's tilapia. They don't serve trout—ever. Why do they have the word trout on their sign, I wonder. I don't ask. I just order the fish, which is ok, but not great.

After we eat, we decide to check out the beach but without high hopes because it's about 50 degrees, rainy, and windy. Needless to say, the beach is dreary; perhaps it's lovely when the sun is shining and the water is blue. It just seems a little trashed, a little neglected. Maybe that's the result of the storm. Our phone apps say this will be the weather all weekend. I've come equipped with my full coverage bathing suit but, clearly, I'm not going to need it. I feel bad because Jon isn't going to get any beach time out of this. Maybe the hotel pool will do. It's indoors, and very nice. Yet, back at the hotel, we find it filled with children, of course, because they can't play on the beach. Cristina's son wisely observes that the pool water is probably about 80% pee at this point. No one, he remarks with a straight-face, not even a child, should be willing to brave that swill. So, we wander around the town to see what it has to offer. Sadly, it's not much. It's kind of run down, kind of dreary, like the beach. There are a few hip-looking bars, and plenty of shops and stalls selling goods for tourists, but not much else to see or do. One of our main purposes in choosing Tecolutla as our vacation destination, however, besides the fact that it's the closest beach town to San Agustín, is that the archeological site of Tajin is only about forty minutes away, back in the direction of Papantla.

Since we all know I don't do well with a lot of sun anyway, I'm pretty thrilled that we'll be exploring the site on a cloudy cool day. Doing it in the blazing heat, which is how the weather usually is in this region, along with high humidity, would be unpleasant. So, we retire to our rooms, looking forward to tomorrow.

This morning, we meet Cristina and her son bright and early at a place that looks basically like a diner, and which seems popular with tourists and locals alike. We have a satisfying breakfast of ham, eggs, pancakes, and that sort of thing, always with plenty of fresh tortillas on the side. After gathering up our adventure gear, we pile in the car and drive back along the river, through the busy town, onto the highway lined with exotic tropical vegetation, bypassing the center of Papantla toward Tajín.

Between the parking lot and the official entrance to the site, there is the usual corridor of *tchotchkes*, including traditional-looking embroidered clothes. I'm still looking for another dress for my child's partner, who told me she wants a white Mexican dress, embroidered with flowers. Cristina tells me not to buy it here. She says that in these places they are likely not made by local people but could even be from China! Good to know.

We pay the entrance fee and head into the park and along the path, which, in minutes, opens out onto the grounds. There, five or six huge pyramids rise into the sky, built of the dark-looking stone of the region, very different from the light-colored rock of Tula. These pyramids are magnificent. You can't climb on them because the stone is slowly deteriorating, but seeing them from the ground is awe-inspiring. I'm always humbled by these places, built by people of great intelligence and ingenuity, belonging to complex civilizations long in the past. I think of the sacredness they represent, and those sacrificed in the name of their gods.

If you haven't been to Teotihuacan, just outside of Mexico City and probably the most famous archeological site in Mexico with the possible exception of Chichén Itzá in the Yucatán, you must make that a destination. I mention it here because you can actually climb to the top of the pyramids of Teotihuacan, and they are immense. The pyramids here in Tajín, a total of fourteen over the entire, enormous site, aren't as big, but they are of a completely different design. I don't know how many archeological sites there are in Mexico with pyramids, because the number hasn't been documented—needless to say, a lot—more than you can probably ever visit. Tajín is one of the lesser-known sites outside of Mexico but it's really worth seeing. It remained undiscovered until the 1970's when a casual hiker stumbled upon it. Can you imagine a place the size of several football fields, sporting fourteen large pyramids, could remain unnoticed nearby a fairly large town? Imagine the surprise of that lone hiker. Just so you know, this place is about four hours from San Agustín, and about three and a half from Mexico City.

Once we've seen all there is to see, we get some snacks from the vendors who hang out in certain sections of the park, and marvel at hearing them speak their native language to each other. On the way out, Jon buys a t-shirt, of course, and then we get back in the car and head toward the center of Papantla. I'm hungry now, in spite of the snacks but, because of the snacks, my stomach hurts. Cristina attempts to ditch the tour of Papantla, genuinely worried that I might be dying on her watch, but the streets are crowded, and it takes a while to wind our way out of the town and on the road back to Tecolutla.

Once there, after some rest, I feel better, and am now really hungry. We meet Cristina and her son back at that same diner, where Cristina refuses to let us pay, even though I offered first.

Aside from her bit of stubbornness, there are so many amazing things about Cristina, other than the fact that she's a brilliant scientist. One of them is that she not only loves children—all children—but makes a point of talking to all the little ones who come to our table to sell things as they do in a tourist town. She never talks down to them, but looks directly in their eyes (perhaps she chooses to use her diminutive stature for this purpose because she does it so very effectively) and speaks to them in the most natural way. She always gives them a few pesos, even though she doesn't buy what they're selling. One little boy is seriously crippled. After he limps away, she remarks that he probably had polio. I have a moment of panic in having been in such close proximity to him because, even though we've all had our immunizations, it's been like a hundred years. Do they last all that time? I guess so. Then I feel ashamed of myself for feeling that way and my fear turns to sadness that there are still people in the world who don't have access to polio vaccines. Others, perhaps from lack of education, won't get them.

After dinner, we tell the hotel receptionist we won't be staying another night. There's no point. There's nothing to do here while the weather is so bad and it will be for at least another day. We can't get a refund with such a late cancellation, but we can get a credit for another stay. It's clear that Jon and I won't be returning but Cristina says she might bring her family again. Even though she agrees that the town isn't great, even in good weather, at least it's a beach. I'd probably feel very differently about the place if it had been nice enough to swim in the ocean. And so, we give our credit to her. I hope she ends up using it.

This morning, after breakfast, we head back to San Agustín. It's foggy as we go through the mountains, which makes me a little nervous, but Cristina is an excellent driver and has good music to boot. Our conversation ranges to all kinds of topics and, inevitably, turns to politics. I discover that Cristina likes to stay neutral about most political topics, except for how much she hates Mexico's current president, Andrés Manuel López Obrador, or AMLO as they call him. AMLO is on the far left, and Cristina seems like she's pretty progressive even though she says she's neutral. Still, she thinks he's an idiot and hates what he's doing to the country. I have a dear friend in Mexico City named Cecilia, someone I've known nearly all my life (more about that soon) who is definitely on the conservative side so of course hates AMLO. Yet, I've come to find out that conservative people here are generally quite progressive socially, as is Cecilia. I would describe Marco's dad, Fernando, as conservative, as he believes the poor are getting hand-outs from AMLO's government, so, of course, he hates him, but he also hates the conservative faction of the U.S. government that was recently in power. Rico, who strikes me as conservative in spirit though he is, socially, extremely liberal, voted for AMLO, and now deeply regrets it. In fact, I have yet to meet one Mexican person from any walk of life who supports AMLO.

That topic leads to others and we end up talking about racism. Cristina shares about how she was in Germany a few years ago with some other Mexican people and experienced devastating prejudice there. As I mentioned, Cristina is small and very dark skinned, quite native looking, in fact. She says there she felt threatened more than once as people hurled slurs at her that she didn't understand, and gave her looks she definitely did. It breaks my heart that someone as brilliant and lovely and compassionate as Cristina would ever be treated badly for any reason, but especially for her race. It's the perfect example of people judging others by how they look, rather than by the content of their character to paraphrase MLK. How dare they treat my friend like that.

Perhaps trying to express my solidarity, I remark that I would trade my white skin for dark because I think it's more beautiful, adding that it would be nice to fit in in Mexico and not stand out as I do. She retorts that if I had experienced what she did, I wouldn't trade my skin color for anything. That shuts me up. Of course she's right. What a stupid thing to say. I have no idea what it's like to experience racism of any kind. My life has been nothing but privilege.

From Jon:

Guard dog rooftop copper and clay

Iron art windows wrought over glass

Sun soaked garden gates towering high

Shattered bottle top walls barbed and defended insecurely secure

Bright brick patterned porticos spilling music to the street

But for the shadows Mexico is color

Frida y La Virgen together painting the world

Fire spark glow patina jeweled celebration

Legends and destiny twirl in the clouds

Children of warriors palms raised

seeking relief and recognition

But for the shadows Mexico is color

Fields of maíz wave to the wind spiraling silk

Wild plants springing from sidewalks untended life

Flower pots flowing, budding, blooming to blossoming bright

Bougainvillea contemplating palm, pine, papaya, coconut, and plantain alike

But for the shadows Mexico is color

Ancient language on new lips stories of grandeur and loss

Bouquets pushed to car glass chicles for sale

Tianguis swirling ebb and flow the river of trade

Spice cinnamon, garlic, cebolla, apples, toys, dresses, sparkle lights, bits of string, and pulque... pulque

The color is joy, honor, friendship, family and strangers as one

But for the shadows Mexico is color

Mariachis call loudly the beauty of song longing and triumph

Silver star buttons on velvet night skies rising beyond moons

Sunrise roosters submit all to the dawn breathing fire and promise

Another day granted a blessing in process

But for the shadows Mexico is color

Red, blue, magenta, orange, violet. An eye-riot welcome and celebration que Viva!

Kaleidoscope walls display ink outlines lampposts, grapevines, stairwells, skylines, rooftops, tents, stages, church bells, spires, and arches.

Mexico is color and shadow

Eternal lovers entwined in the dance of the day

El baile de un día outside of time

2,300,000 to 2,420,000 Steps

Today Cecilia arrives from Mexico City for a visit, so let me fill you in with some background. Ceci (as most people call her) and I met when we were fifteen. Her younger sister, Cristi, had come up to where my family lived in Tucson for a summer, as a part of an informal exchange between her family and mine. My older sister didn't participate because she didn't speak Spanish, but I'd been learning it in school. Cristi and I became good friends, but when I went to Mexico City the following summer, I met Ceci, and she and I really bonded. The summer after that, when Ceci and I were sixteen, she came to Tucson.

After that, I didn't see her again until almost ten years later, during which time a tragic thing occurred in her family's life. When Cristi was about twenty-two, she and the oldest girl in their family were killed in a car crash as the family was returning from Acapulco. One of the older sister's children was also injured, but he recovered. When my family received this news, it was almost incomprehensible. To lose not one child, but two in the same instance, and in such a cruel way. Ceci and other members of her family were in one of two cars, the first, and passed a truck on the highway. The second car, with Cristi in it, attempted to pass the truck next, but they didn't make it. I can hardly stand to think about it.

The following summer, or maybe it was two summers later, Ceci came to see my family in Tucson. Then, they all traveled to New York, where I was living at the time, and we went from there to Nova Scotia for a major road/ferry trip, which included Prince Edward Island, Newfoundland, Maine, and New England. After that, Ceci stayed with me for a week before returning home to Mexico to start preparing for her wedding which would be a year later. During those three weeks that Ceci spent with me and my family, we reconnected in a major way. Remember, this was before the internet and long before social media, so it was hard to keep in touch, sending letters back and forth between our countries, and so we didn't much. Yet, those three weeks cemented our bond.

The September after she returned to Mexico, one of the largest earthquakes in modern history struck her city. Fortunately, her family was unscathed, but the damage in terms of life and property was incalculable. The following summer I went to Mexico City for her wedding, a wonderful week of being with her and her family though the loss of the two sisters was palpable, and the memory of the earthquake sharp. As a result, the wedding was more like a funeral service.

After that, we really did lose touch. I got married a few years later but neither she nor her family members were able to attend. She had her first baby, and a few years later had a second girl. Eventually, she and her husband got divorced and then I lost her, or so I thought. Though her parents still lived at their same address, she didn't, and I never knew if any cards or letters I sent were forwarded to her.

Then, a miracle occurred in the form of Facebook. It was my brother who dug her up on the site and connected with her, and then put her in touch with me. It was a way to communicate again and, then, of course, we could exchange emails.

Sometime in the mid-2000s her daughters came to New York and, though they didn't stay with us, we met them on a few occasions and were totally charmed by how lovely and intelligent they were.

The next time I saw her was at my twenty-fifth wedding anniversary party in New York. Can you imagine? Nearly thirty years had passed since we'd last seen each other. She came up with her boyfriend at that time, and seeing her was just like it always was—like not a moment had gone by since we'd last been together.

After that, my child was invited to spend a couple of weeks with her and her daughters in Mexico City so the kid got to experience the wonder of that place with those amazing people. In 2018, we all went there for a visit just before I started my master's program in Spanish. At that point, the strong connections between our families were becoming established all over again.

It was vital to give you that background so you understand her importance in my life. I love her like a sister.

Now, here we are, about four years later. She arrives today, Friday, delivered by the gentleman who has been her driver for years. He's going back to Mexico City by himself and, since Jon will be leaving for Las Vegas for his dad's memorial service on Sunday, she'll catch a ride to CDMX with him via taxi.

Though I always felt like I had to apologize to the Americans who came to visit our humble home here, to her, I don't feel that need. She's Mexican so she gets it. Not to say she doesn't live in a very elegant apartment in the city, and was raised as one of the upper class of society, but she knows her country and how people here live. She understands the house's eccentricities but she's charmed by it at the same time. I make her some lunch and then we relax for the afternoon, chatting and catching up. There's no limit to how far our conversation can reach.

Later, we go out to explore San Agustín. I figure that, as a sophisticated city person, she'll find it all very provincial, but she loves it: the church, the plaza, the daily marketplace, everything. In fact, she comments that San Agustín is the authentic Mexican town that everyone, including Mexicans, is looking for.

This evening we go to La Hacienda for dinner and José comes by to join us for a while, as is his habit. Maybe Teresa wasn't entirely his type but Ceci seems to be. He asks what she does for a living and she tells him she's a motivational speaker for corporations, and a life coach for individuals. (She is considered one of the best in the business. I've seen her videos—I can vouch for it.) He's quite interested in this and suggests she come back and do a talk for his workers, friends, and family members at the restaurant. They exchange information and I wonder if this isn't a ruse on his part to have an excuse to be in touch with her. After he leaves our table, I ask if she could be interested in him and she gives me a decided no. He's very nice, not entirely unattractive, but he's not her type. "Not rich enough," she jokes.

Today is Saturday and we've decided to check out a nearby town which is referred to by locals, and by a sign on the highway, as "The Mural Place."

When we lived in New York, Jon had the idea to gather artists to paint the graffiti-tagged walls in our somewhat run-down neighborhood with mural art to beautify it and discourage more tagging. A friend of ours connected us with artists who knew lots of muralists, and they organized the first installment of what came to be called the "Welling Court Mural Project." It continued, year after year, expanding and expanding until the entire neighborhood became a sought-after New York City art destination. To this day, eight years after we left New York, it continues, a legacy we're proud to have left behind.

Naturally, we're extremely interested in seeing this "mural place," and have been waiting for just the right moment to do it. Having Ceci here is the perfect excuse. After breakfast, we head into the *centro* to track down a taxi. We come across an elderly driver who is game to take us, a fellow named Ismael. We ask if he knows of the mural place, which in Spanish is *el lugar de los murales*. He says, "Sure, of course!" And off we go. He tools off on a route we don't recognize. I ask him about it but he assures us it's the right way. Ceci confirms the name of our destination with him and, again, he insists this is the right way. Jon keeps saying he's taking us in the opposite direction, and I see that, but I figure he must know an alternate route. About fifteen minutes later, we arrive in some little community, and Ismael proclaims, "Here we are, Morales!"

Both Ceci and I respond in Spanish, "No, not Morales, *murales*!"

He has no clue what we're talking about and I'm relieved it wasn't just me he misunderstood.

Now, he listens to us as we give him the right directions. We've known all along, of course, it's just that he seemed so confident. Without any hard feelings, he follows our directions and we eventually get to the sign on the highway that points to the mural place. He's still skeptical so he stops alongside the road to ask a fieldhand wearing a broad sombrero, who confirms we're going the right way.

In just a few minutes more, we arrive in Colonia Morelos (not Morales) and are greeted by the sight of murals on every building in this small town. They are beautiful—absolutely world class mural art—each one with themes significant to Latin culture. As we drive around the town, we see them everywhere we look, on practically every building, including the walls of homes. Where did this mural project come from, we wonder. Who organized it? How did they get the townspeople to agree? Where did the artists come from? I'll have to ask Arlo. He knows everything.

It takes about a half an hour to tour the entire town. We had planned on getting out and walking but we'd never be able to see it all by foot. Even Ismael is amazed. He says he's lived in nearby San Agustín his whole life and has never seen this. I bet he's not the only one.

"This is art!" he exclaims. "This is culture!" He can't wait to bring his son, also a cab driver, to see it with him.

By now, it's around 1:00 so we ask him to take us to the little restaurant where I first met with Cristina, simultaneously called La Cocina and Fusion. I wish it was open for dinner because it's a little more upscale than other places around San Agustín (though not La

Hacienda), but they close at 5:00 every day. When Ismael drops us off, he quotes us 200 pesos for the hour he's been with us, which is only about ten dollars. I give him 250 and thank him, though he seems more grateful to us for showing him such a wonderful place.

Today, Jon and Ceci leave at 9:00 for CDMX with Antonio, the faithful cab driver who drove us to and from Actopan a couple of times (Ismael doesn't go as far as Mexico City). The visit with Ceci has been stupendous and I'm hoping to see her again before we go home, especially since she very well may end up giving a talk at La Hacienda in a few weeks. It's strange to be alone in this house with just Lupita, but I have a party to go to tonight in the courtyard for Claudio's birthday, something I'm very much looking forward to.

Last night's party was great: lots of grilled meats, yummy desserts, and the pleasure of Miriam, Maya, Claudio and their lovely extended family. I wonder why they never invite Marco and his family to these affairs which probably has to do with their mothers' feuding. I am aware, however, that right now, Marco's dad, Fernando, is about to have a cancerous tumor removed from his kidney and their family is very wrapped up in this with good reason. I, too, am worried about Fernando.

This morning I wake up to no hot water. The starter on the boiler seems to be broken. I text Marco in the most thoughtful way possible because I know he is dealing with his dad's situation. He responds that he can't be bothered right now. I gently remind him that I'm completely without hot water and can't he suggest someone to fix it? He says no, he can't. I again gently remind him that Jon is out of town for his own father's funeral, that I am also mourning, and that I need for him to at least give me the name of someone to call. He ignores me.

It's been four days with no hot water. The only response I've gotten from Marco is that he doesn't know who to call. Miriam finally suggests I try the guy that fixed our Christmas plumbing situation though I didn't think this was a plumber problem. I get ahold of him this morning and he comes and replaces the starter on the boiler. It was very simple.

I'm feeling pretty upset with Marco right now and am starting to realize why he and his cousin aren't always on good terms. The longer we've been his tenants, the less attention he's paid to the house—the house that shares a courtyard with that cousin. Figuring he's never been a landlord before, I once mentioned to him that it's a landlord's responsibility to fix things that go wrong that aren't the tenants' fault. He obviously doesn't see it that way. I wondered if this is how things are in Mexico but Ceci assured me it is not. This most recent exchange between me and him has left me feeling angry and disappointed. As much as Jon and I don't want to leave San Agustín, and probably would have been content to continue renting this place in our absence so that we could return to it in the future, we're now starting to look forward to getting back to our nice home in Portland. We still don't want to say good-bye to San Agustín but, with only two months left, that reality is starting to weigh on us. In some ways, Marco is making it easier to confront.

From Jon: my journey to Las Vegas, NV, for my dad's memorial service was what one might expect. Major culture shock and general chaos. When I went from my hotel to the house that now belongs to my sister, I walked. Everyone there was astounded that I would do such a thing. It's so far, they declared. They could not know that, for me, it was many thousand fewer steps than I would have taken on any normal day in San Agustín. I didn't bother to explain.

As for my dad, my relationship with him was something of an ongoing battle until I left home at seventeen and stopped speaking to him for about five years. As far as I could tell while growing up, he was a crazy man. I didn't understand PTSD and neither did he nor anyone around him. Things do come into focus through that lens. When we finally reunited, he began to see me as an equal, which helped a lot.

Something else that caused our relationship to solidify was my having an epiphany while driving in my car one day. I drove straight to his appliance repair shop in North Hollywood and dragged him away from his "important work" to a local diner, where I told him the reality of my life up to that point, including all the craziness that you can imagine a young man getting up to in Southern California in the seventies. He told me about what his life was like after the war when I was a kid who couldn't possibly understand his confusion, despair and rage. Bottom line: we bonded. He was still crazy but, finally, at that late date, we had each other's back. I was twenty-five years old. Better late than never. That bond continued to the day of his death. Like I said, he was indeed crazy, but I was able to see through that to his clear sense of right and wrong, his kindness, his generosity, and his love of family. No matter where I was in the world, we spoke often. When he died, we were clean. The last couple years of his life were difficult for him, but he never let the opportunity pass to tell me that he loved me and Georgina, whom he adored, and our child. I never missed that opportunity to reciprocate. The funeral was a simple one, with few people there. A simple plaque on the ground next to my mother's marks the location of his ashes. Neither he, nor my mother, are there. They have both moved on. The trumpets of the honor guard provided by the military were sincere though brief. A lot of soldiers of that era are now passing away in large numbers and, like the boot camps they were hurried through on their way to war, their final goodbyes are, of a necessity, short. I had said my goodbyes and thank yous to him many times whenever we had the opportunity to speak while I was in Mexico. We both knew his time was coming. He often let me know that he did not fear death. When he left this world, he finally had the peace that had evaded him much of his life. He did his best. All anyone can do.

I returned to San Agustín the next day. It was good to go home.

2,420,000 to 2,470,000 Steps

Jon has had just one day to get his bearings after getting back from Las Vegas. It was a rather difficult trip for him considering the circumstances. He also said he experienced that same culture shock I did in La Paz—worse, though, because he was fully in the U.S. This makes me worry about what it will be like for us when we go home.

But today is not the day to think about that because we're off to Oaxaca. In all the time I've spent in Mexico, this is a place I've never gotten to visit though I've heard incredible things about it. We've also gotten lots of advice from friends here in San Agustín about what to see and do there though we only have three days in which to do it. This will be the longest we've had to leave Lupita and I know she'll be upset, but Miriam and Maya are on the job.

I call a different driver to take us to the airport because Antonio is ridiculously late. This other driver gets us there in good time, though, once we figure out where to go in the airport and get through security, we're just in time to board the flight. We've got everything stuffed into two backpacks because we can only take one personal item each though I see others getting on with more so I guess the airline is pretty lax about that. It's just a one-hour flight to Oaxaca City. Once there, we get in line for transport vans that take you where you want to go in the town. You can't get a taxi from the airport—or even an Uber—they're just not allowed.

The van takes forever to drop the various passengers off at their destinations and finally delivers us to ours, a cute little boutique hotel I found online that is just as nice as I'd hoped. Once we deposit our stuff, we go off to find dinner. The girl at the front desk has directed us to the center of town, just about a ten-minute walk. We follow her directions, down a cobblestone hill, to a hip-looking area with a few dinner options. We choose a restaurant that looks promising, and I have delicious *flautas*, while Jon opts for a salad (rather brave if you ask me).

On the way back to the hotel, we pass a place that looks like a fancy nightclub. There's a drop-dead beautiful trans person outside selling tickets so we ask them what it's all about. They say it's a sensory-theatrical experience, a two-hour, blindfolded excursion of tastes, smells, sounds, and touch, which costs a thousand pesos each. It's full tonight, they say, since only ten people are allowed in at a time. We actually consider it for tomorrow, until we realize we have so much to see and do here, we don't really want to spend two hours and the equivalent of one hundred dollars tasting and smelling weird stuff with our eyes closed.

Today, we want to simply explore the city. We start with an excellent breakfast at a café just up the street, then walk along a different route to the main area of town so we can take in the sights. It's sunny and warm out, a little humid, but not too bad. Along the way, we pass an enclosed marketplace with all kinds of foods, prepared and fresh, for sale. Making a note of it, we continue on to the historic center, where the cathedral of Santo Domingo reigns. By the way, it's holy week; Palm Sunday, in fact, and everywhere in the town you see purple and white *papel picado* strung across the streets. They flutter in the breeze, making everything seem even more festive.

This town is packed with beautiful architecture, colonial-style for sure, but all the buildings are painted in bright colors, with exquisite mural art on many walls. It's definitely not the place to go to avoid tourists because they are everywhere and from everywhere. I notice, though, that when I begin conversations in Spanish with store owners or vendors or whomever, they happily continue in their native language even though many here speak English well. I'm glad people don't treat me like your typical American, due, I'm sure, to my ease with Spanish and my desire to communicate in it exclusively. There's no avoiding the fact that we're tourists in this town, however, so we may as well embrace it.

As we meander past the cathedral, overflowing with Palm Sunday celebrants, I remain vigilant for an umbrella since I figured one would be easy to find here. The sun is hot and I will need something soon but, so far, I haven't seen any. We wander through various marketplaces—Oaxaca is famous for them. I'm also looking for a particular type of blouse, a nice leather purse, and we definitely want to find artisanal chocolate. We were told to go to this one place, Mayordomo, for chocolate. Artisanal it might be, but it turns out to have kind of a factory vibe, as the workers there churn out chocolates for the tourists to snap up. We buy some to distribute to family and friends at home but I was hoping for something less commercial.

From Jon: For all their attempt at blatant commercialism with their "modern" approach to selling their chocolate, we were quite surprised upon tasting it later to discover that everything was mislabeled. That was laughable if a bit disappointing, but life goes on. It's only chocolate. What am I saying!? It does need to be said, I did have a cool and refreshing chocolate drink from the same place, which my chocolate gene responded to with great enthusiasm.

There is a lot of the downtown area to explore in Oaxaca, and we walk as far and see as much as possible before we start to wear out. An unusual sight catches our eye as we go, an occupation of a hundred tents in the middle of what must usually be a busy intersection, set up and organized well, and also very clean. I'm thinking it's probably not homeless people, but I don't quite understand the jargon on the signs they have strung up. Clearly, it's a protest, but I'm not sure about what.

At this point, my desperation for an umbrella has turned to settling for a hat. I don't like to wear hats because they smush down my hair, but this is becoming an *emergency*. There are lots of vendors selling these kinds of straw, Indiana Jones-type hats, so I finally buy one with a pretty flower design painted on it, from a young woman with a stack of them to sell.

After that we make our way back to the restaurant we ate at last night and, for lunch, I have chicken enchiladas in black mole, which is just about the most wonderful thing I've ever eaten. Jon has one of the famous dishes of Oaxaca, the *tlalyuda*, a gigantic tortilla type of thing filled with Oaxacan cheese and black beans. It's also delicious but way too big to eat, so we take the leftovers home with us. Oaxaca is known for its world class cuisine—some of the best in Mexico—and we're starting to see why.

After a nap at the hotel and time just lazing around, we head back into the city at around 4:00. Even this late in the afternoon, it's almost too hot but, with limited time in the city, we need to make the most of it. We wander back to the downtown to see if there are more marketplaces to discover. Actually, there are two huge marketplaces we're interested in seeing: the Mercado Benito Juarez, and the Mercado 20 de Noviembre. It turns out they're not hard to find because they're gigantic and in the middle of everything—I don't know how we missed them yesterday.

Though it's late in the day and the stalls are starting to close up, we first check out the Mercado Benito Juarez to see if I can find any of the items on my list. The place is immense—you could seriously get lost in there. Failing to find a blouse or a purse to my taste, we exit, to find that the Mercado 20 de Noviembre is right across the street. While the Benito Juarez market is for artisanal wares and that kind of thing, the other is all food. In fact, Miriam told us that the best places to eat in Oaxaca are in the marketplaces. This one is overwhelming, hundreds of little restaurants, trying to draw you in for a meal, all specializing in *tlayudas*. It's hot in there, and smoky, though there's one part of the market that's especially so, where you go if what you want is grilled meats. It's so smoky in that area the air is thick and dark with it. This is not where we want to dine on a hot evening. We actually have in mind something a bit nicer. We leave the market and head back in the direction of the main plaza where the church is. We step into one restaurant, but the menu does not inspire, so we leave and keep wandering. When we reach the plaza, we notice there are some rooftop restaurants around the periphery that look nice. We gravitate to one and go up the stairs to find just the place we had been looking for. With the breeze blowing cool now, this shady oasis has a spectacular view of the church and plaza, and a menu full of delicious sounding things.

The food is, indeed, wonderful. I have seared tuna and Jon has a steak. Jon declares that the margarita he ordered is one of the best he's ever had—so of course he has two. The service is excellent, the atmosphere divine, and we are falling in love with Oaxaca.

After we finish, we take a peek inside the cathedral, but it's still packed with church goers, having had services every hour on the hour throughout the day.

We take a cab home because it's all uphill. The driver is a really nice guy, so we ask if we can reserve him to bring us to the archeological site we plan to visit tomorrow, Monte Albán. He says of course and we end the evening contented as can be with this amazing place, and the promise of more tomorrow.

We head out at 10:00 this morning, after a breakfast of scrambled eggs on the hotel rooftop. Our driver takes us up a hill overlooking Oaxaca City to Monte Albán. It's a hot day and I'm glad I have my hat. After perusing the indoor museum of artifacts, we climb to the top of the site from where you can overlook the original pre-Hispanic city. It's brown and barren at this time of year, but boasts about six large pyramids and some other structures. This site is impressive in its sheer size and design, but it's not as complete as Teotihuacan or Tajín, nor as architecturally interesting as Tula. The pyramids are not incredibly tall and you can climb on some of them, but we choose not to as it's getting hotter by the second. As always, it's amazing to take in the remnants of the ancient civilizations, but we eventually high-tail it to the one shade tree, helpfully, with a bench under it. We rest there and enjoy the view of the site until others come around who look like they could use the bench, and so we vacate. We've arranged with the cab driver to pick us up at 12:00, so we make our way along the desert road that leads back to the entrance, then hike down another road to a parking lot where we agreed to meet him. He's there exactly on time and it's a relief to not be in the sun anymore, though the car, like (as we've now come to terms with), most cabs in Mexico, doesn't have AC.

We have him drop us off at the small marketplace near our hotel so we can grab some lunch. We opt for a stand where we can get sandwiches, or *tortas*, as they're known in Mexico. What we end up with is not all that great to be honest, but it will do because we're hungry. After that, it's definitely naptime at the hotel.

For our late afternoon jaunt, we call our faithful driver and have him deliver us to The Museum of Modern Art, the only museum open on this Monday. As we ride along, we spot two men holding hands. I wonder what his opinion will be of this, but he spots them on his own and declares "*Oaxaca es libre!*" "Oaxaca is free!" I smile to myself.

He has to take a detour to get us to our destination because of the tent occupation. I ask him about it and he tells me it's a teachers' strike, apparently having been there for months. Now, the cleanliness and organization makes sense and I wish for them the resolution they desire. That's the kind of determination you rarely see in occupations or protests in the U.S. Or else the police break them up before they can have too much of an impact.

As a result of the occupation, he has to drop us off a block or so from the museum. Once we get there and pay the admission, we realize it's not very interesting. I've heard there are some great museums in Oaxaca, but this isn't one of them. Architecturally, it's beautiful, but the art is rather ho-hum. Still, it offers some shady tables where we can sit and cool off for a while.

Now that the evening is coming on and it's becoming more comfortable outside, we set off in search of a neighborhood I've read about called Jalatlaco. Apparently, it has some great mural art on display and is supposedly a hipster haven. I don't care about the hipster part, but I figure we might find a good spot for dinner there. It takes us about fifteen minutes, a lovely walk, enjoying the colorful and structurally pleasing houses along the way. We know when we've reached Jalatlaco because of the mural art that frames the entrance to the neighborhood. The streets are cobbled, the shops cute, but no restaurants catch our eye other than taco joints.

We're interested in experiencing more of the unique Oaxacan food yet, as we continue to walk toward the center of town, our search for the right restaurant isn't yielding anything. Finally, we come across a place that looks nice and we enter to find a big space, rather elegant, with nothing but empty tables. The waiter assures us they're open, and we figure this is as good as it's going to get unless we head back to the main plaza and the place we ate at last night. The food isn't quite as good, but there are local specialties on the menu and I end up with pasta with Oaxacan cream and mushrooms particular to that area. It's delicious.

From Jon: one of the things peculiar to Mexico in general is their attachment to TV. Everywhere we go, be it in San Agustín or here in Oaxaca, TVs adorn the walls and are often tuned to telenovelas (Mexican Soap Operas) or music. In this particular place the required TV is tuned to a music station and they're playing "Pump Up the Jam" which is a Belgian band's contribution to the 90's (released by Technotronic in 1989). We find this quite hilarious because we've been randomly watching Cunk on Earth *on Netflix. If you know, you know.*

Laughter, as is often the case for us, is a welcome and delicious part of our meal.

Since this is our last evening here, I'm determined to find the blouse I have in mind so, on our way back to the plaza, we check out some pop-up markets along the way. And there it is: rust orange, not too showy, with a little embroidery, authentic looking but not too touristy. I snap it up. I still haven't found the purse of my dreams though. I take that back. I did find it, in a shop near our hotel, where a guy makes all the leather goods himself. This simple bag of dark brown leather is perfect, but a little pricey, so I've been thinking about it. On the way home, we stop by the shop, I make my decision and buy it. This will be a true treasure from Mexico, and Oaxaca in particular.

This morning, we have breakfast with one of my fellow Fulbright ETAs who just got into town with her mother. I recommended the hotel to them, and so we meet in the lobby and walk over to the restaurant we've eaten at twice and really loved. This young woman is one of the best and brightest of the program, a person I connected with at the orientation last August. She's a true leader and I know she will go far in life. Her mother is just as lovely, and we enjoy our last meal in Oaxaca with them before our driver comes to pick us up and deliver us to the airport. Apparently, cabs can arrive with passengers, they just can't pick them up there.

And so, we say good-bye to Oaxaca, a city we've come to adore. It was way too short a time here, but we pledge to be back for much longer a visit. If you go nowhere else in Mexico, go to Oaxaca City.

From Jon:
The Shining Land
Flowing verde
Verdant
Lush
Corn maíz
hñähñu neon
Sun's children
Quiet
Proud
In constant
Struggle to embrace
Greatness
Leaning on soap
Day-lit bubbles
Caught in amber
Pulse rápido
Stilled
Without notice
Expecting
Breathless
Paused
Spark-fire glow
Glistening
Waiting
In time
Música
Revolution
Qué viva!
Revelatory
Prosperity seeding

Fire
Images planted
Creative harvest
Arriving
Out there
Just over there
Beyond the horizon
Sunrise

2,470,000 to 2,590,000 Steps

Semana Santa means lots of time off for me. At the end of the week, we witness more than one procession of pilgrims carrying crosses and other icons through the streets with great reverence. Good Friday happens to be my child's birthday this year, but we can't do more than text them as they work at their club all weekend. Early next week we'll do a Facetime.

Easter Sunday we attend mass, which takes place outside in the huge courtyard in front of the church as they can accommodate many more people there on folding chairs, under a great tent. It starts with Mariachis, which is promising, but then becomes a typical mass. We leave about ten minutes in. It's just not interesting to us though I appreciate the sacredness of the occasion and how meaningful it is to the people of this community and to Mexicans in general.

Monday I'm still off, and students seem to be on their own vacations this week.

Teachers are doing evaluations this week—now the third week of April—and don't need me. Rico is going out of town for several days, and has asked me to fill in for him in the office since this is a time when students will be coming by to get their TOEFL (Test of English as a Foreign Language) results. I'm happy to do it. I like the idea of hanging out in the office by myself with time to work on my Mother's Day presentation and do some writing of my own. Rico trains me on how to look up students in his system, find their results, and certify them.

Today, Monday, I hate to have to inform Rico via text that I'm sick as a dog. Jon and I ate at La Cocina yesterday, where we've never had a single problem but I'm pretty sure it's the culprit. My stomach was hurting last night so we had some simple pasta for dinner but, by about midnight, there was no keeping anything down. I hurled like I haven't hurled in years, which is so disgusting. I'm sorry to have to share it with you but I feel like it's one of those details, and realities of Mexico that one has to accept. I had eaten my favorite meal, enchiladas, at the restaurant, smothered in cilantro. Jon didn't have any because he's allergic (kind of an inconvenience in Mexico). What I suspect is that either the cilantro wasn't disinfected properly or that the women who work there were distracted by taking care of the baby who hangs out in a playpen near the kitchen (something you'd never see in the States), and maybe forgot to wash their hands after they changed his diaper or whatever. I texted Cristina about it and she confirmed: e. coli. That signals poop, people, poop. Gross.

The rest of the week I was able to be in the office and it truly was fun and relaxing. If I needed to take a break, I'd put a sign on the door to let the students know I'd be back later. I had enough students come by to make me feel useful; in fact, I liked the official feeling of it—I was Rico for the week and sort of came to understand the appeal of his job.

In general, school seems to be winding down for the rest of my time here. May 1st is the Mexican version of Labor Day, so we have that day off, and May 5th, of course, is Cinco de Mayo so there's no working that day. The days in between are rather superfluous. Hopefully, you know the history but, if not, let me be clear. Cinco de Mayo is not the Mexican Independence Day as some people think. It is the day the Mexicans won the Battle of Puebla against the French invading army and, I may add, against all odds, as the French army was very well prepared and organized.

Before that week unfolds, however, we get to enjoy another visit, today, April 29th, from Cecilia. Tomorrow is the day of her presentation at La Hacienda. She arrives via her driver whom she puts up at La Casa Azul hotel. We spend the afternoon in our usual chat-fest, and I make dinner at home. The problem is, she hasn't heard from José in a week or so and wants to be sure everything is in place for tomorrow. After dinner, we go by the restaurant. As soon as José sees her, he expresses great relief because he's lost his phone and couldn't get in touch with her. He said he even came by our house and rang the bell but we must have been out wandering around the plaza at the time. Anyway, we enjoy some drinks and snacks courtesy of José, who also made sure Ceci's driver received a nice meal.

This morning Ceci heads over there about 9:00, and we follow at 10:00, which is when the event is supposed to start. Of course, it starts nowhere near 10:00. Everyone is served breakfast, which I've already eaten, and that takes extra time. Then, they can't get her Power Point presentation hooked up to the TV monitors. Finally, they get it worked out and Ceci launches into what she does, expertly, I may add. She gives an inspirational talk to José's workers and family, which includes a contingent of nuns, focused on how to achieve what you want in life by taking responsibility for the things that happen to you, and not to blame your lack of success or happiness on other people. I think it's a message a lot of people probably need to hear. There is much more to it and I take copious notes, as do the nuns, I notice, because all of it is good advice. I'm starving by the time she finishes a couple of hours later so I go out to get *pastes* for lunch, so she can have them when she gets back because I know she'll be hungry. Her driver then takes her back to Mexico City before the traffic sets in, but it's been a great couple of days with her, especially getting to see, live and in person, what she does for a living, and does so amazingly well.

Yesterday was Sunday, May 7th, our anniversary. To celebrate, since Rico decided I should have Mondays instead of Fridays off this quarter, Jon and I take a taxi today to a hot springs called Tlaco, between Progreso and Ixmiquilpan. This is a good time to mention we traveled to Ixmiquilpan about a month ago to check out their *tianguis*, which occurs on a Tuesday every week. We've been looking for an artisanal tablecloth to bring home and Miriam said we'd find it there.

Ixmiquilpan is a large and very congested city. It was even more congested within the enormous street market that goes on for blocks and blocks, most of which we traversed without finding said tablecloth. I've heard the city has a fine university and a beautiful ecological park in its center, as well as its being the hub of the Valle del Mezquital, and cradle of the hñähñu people, which seem to be thriving there. All of this was fairly lost on us the day we went to find the tablecloth, however, as we gave up on the *tianguis* and caught a cab to the bus station, where we hopped a bus to Actopan. Though the scenery was spectacular, it was a hot ride and, as usual, I was starving, so we headed straight to El Itacate, which means "food" in hñähñu, a restaurant that is quickly taking the place of La Hacienda as our favorite. They serve local, regional, and indigenous fare, and it is exquisite.

Anyway, our cab driver today is Melquiades, a really nice guy who says he'll wait for us for an hour (or as long as we want, really) at the hot spring, and take us back to San Agustín, all for a reasonable price. We accept this offer, as it doesn't look like there's any other way to get home from here. Tlaco is basically devoid of people, as it's a Monday at 10:00 AM, so we have the large pools of sparkling blue, hot water to ourselves. It is bliss. We just linger the hour, and Melquiades is there on time to take us home though he says he managed to get a fare to and back from Progeso in the meantime, which makes us happy. When we get back to San Agustín, we offer to buy him *pastes* as it's lunchtime. He tells us that his favorite *paste* place is just outside of a big, warehouse store that Jon and I refer to as the big, big store—lots of merchandise, none of it particularly useful.

The *paste* stand always looks closed so we've never tried it but, in fact it is open, and a lovely trans person serves us. The *pastes* are good.

Wednesday, May 10th is Mexican Mother's Day, celebrated by everyone in town bringing flowers to their moms, aunts, grandmothers, and anyone else who qualifies. I'm sure the myriad flower shops love these holidays. I get a big bouquet for Anna and her mom, but they're not there when we bring them so we leave them with the cleaning lady.

Speaking of cleaning ladies, I haven't yet shared the fact that, about two months ago, we hired the lady who cleans Miriam's house, whom they call Doña Angelica. For some reason, we never saw her until one day she was cleaning up the courtyard. It turns out she is the cleaning lady of everyone's dreams. For about fifteen bucks in American dollars, a good wage here, she spends a minimum of five hours (meaning she takes as long as she damn well pleases) cleaning and polishing every square inch of the house and doing things you never thought to do yourself. Though I consider myself a good housekeeper, I'm sure Doña Angelica thinks I'm slovenly compared to how she does it. She gets the floors so shiny they finally look good! And all with white vinegar and water which they don't tend to use here. I only wished I had found her six months earlier.

Today, I do my Mother's Day presentation at school, which focuses on the history of Mother's Day in the U.S. and around the world, and what it means to be a mother in different parts of the globe. I find it meaningful but I don't think it goes over as well as my other presentations have.

One of our U.S. Mother's Day celebrations (or rather just an excuse to go), is a day trip to Mineral del Chico, another of the Magical Towns of Hidalgo. Today, Saturday, we take the usual bus to Pachuca, then a taxi to Mineral, and encounter what is a very small town, pretty as can be, but rather devoid of anything to do other than look at the church and poke into a few shops. After that, all there is left is to have some lunch on a balcony overlooking the plaza, then catch a combi back to Pachuca, and a taxi from there. I'm not saying it was disappointing, but it would have been better if we had had our own car to come and go with because then we could have enjoyed the nearby ecological park which is really what the town and area is known for. It just wasn't possible to do with the limited transportation available to us.

Sunday we have dinner at El Itacate in Actopan.

May is moving along at a clip. There are now a little fewer than two weeks before we leave and I'm feeling despondent. How can I leave this place and our dear friends here, how?

In anticipation of that day, we're starting to give stuff away: clothes and plants for now, but we will ultimately give away all our small appliances, the Talavera dishes, any of the food staples we haven't eaten, tools, art supplies, some of the art we've created, and some blankets. Everything else we'll leave for Marco, as we agreed, but he doesn't get to have all the stuff in the house. Frankly, as a landlord, he hasn't earned it.

Today, May 16th, there is a huge parade in town, of all the students and teachers from all educational institutions. We are required to wear white shirts, blue pants, and a straw hat. I have all these things, the hat being the one I bought in Oaxaca. I get to the meeting place, a large high school that I have trouble finding, to join with everyone else from UPFIM and every other school in town, to line up for our place in the parade. UPFIM is last. It takes about two hours, all of us waiting in the hot sun, until it's finally our turn. By this time, it's around 1:00 and I'm wilting. I march until we get close to the center of town and then I bail. I've got to eat something, soon, and my water has run out. I'm not going to let this be a repeat of the Day of the Dead competition. Later, Rico texts me to find out what happened to me and I tell him it was just too much sun.

2,590,000 to 2,730,000 Steps

The last two weeks of our time in San Agustín flew by. I write this the day after we got home to Portland.

I went back to teaching a more or less normal schedule after the first week in May, though I no longer had my English workshop. Also, I'm sorry to say my writing workshop rather fell apart. Cristina got really busy with her classes and research, and didn't have the time to devote to it any more. I could have carried on without her, but she was performing a key component in it which relied on computer technology I couldn't provide, since my computer couldn't hook up to the projector in the classroom. So, I had her message the students that whoever completed their writing project and turned it in to me would receive full credit for the workshop and get their certificate. (I've collected seven certificates in all during my time here, for the presentations I've done, teaching workshops I've participated in, and for judging the Day of the Dead competition.) I ended up with seven students' projects from the writing workshop, including Cristina's recipe booklet. To view them, go here https://writingworkshoptepatepec.blogspot.com/

The Saturday after my Mother's Day presentation, we went to another baptism party with Arlo. This time, we were prepared. I wore a dress, Jon wore a dress-shirt and slacks, and we brought a present, even though we didn't know the family at all. It was great fun, but we left with Arlo and Fabricio on the early side.

I also want to mention that for the past couple of months, Arlo had been trying to round up a house for us to buy in San Agustín in spite of the fact that there is, basically, no real estate market there. People may slap a For Sale sign on their house but they have no intention of showing it. There are plenty of vacant houses but, as we found out, they mostly belong to grandparents who have passed, leaving kids who are too sentimental to want to sell them. Many times, kids move into those houses themselves but, often as not, since the property tax is so low there, they just leave it to molder. Anyway, we couldn't really afford to buy a house in Mexico at the time, no matter how inexpensive they might have been. Dreaming is always a good thing though. It's something we've always done and, often enough, dreams do come true.

On the 19th, we attended a *Charreada*, something this area is very famous for—essentially, a rodeo. I don't like rodeos, but one of my students assured me it was nothing like a rodeo and that we had to go. I thought it was going to be more of a pageant, with beautiful horses and riders in beautiful costumes performing a beautiful and complex show. No. It was just a rodeo, and a dusty and cold one at that. People sit in this enormous arena, on freezing-cold cement risers for hours, drinking warm beer, eating salty, hot-sauce drenched snacks, watching horses and riders doing the same tricks over and over. I guess it's a competition. We left after an hour. I feel kind of bad that we didn't appreciate it more, because it's an iconic part of the culture, especially of San Agustín's culture and history but, shallow Americans that we are, we were bored beyond belief.

The next day, Miriam and Claudio hosted a farewell party for us in the patio. It was actually our idea, because we wanted to invite all our friends for one final hurrah. We paid for the food and the rented tables and chairs, Claudio manned the grill, and we ate the wonderful barbecued meat that he makes, along with fresh tortillas and guacamole. I had made the guacamole but Miriam beefed it up because, apparently, it was too boring. She made her wonderful chocolate cake for Jon, and an orange pound cake for me.

Not everyone we invited came, but Arlo and his mom were there, some of Claudio and Miriam's friends, Claudio's parents whom we've come to love, Maya and a friend, Anna, her husband and son, and Topiltzin, the guy that Jon met in our first week here, who drove him around looking for a place to rent.

Chula went on the roof again, we blasted music, and had a wonderful time. I wish Cristina and Rico and their families could have come, but they were busy.

On a separate occasion, we invited Gabriela and Antonio, the couple who sells things in the *tianguis*, to have dinner with us. I made a lasagna, which Gabriela loves, and she brought chicken with green mole. We sat around and chatted for a long time, then sent them home with one of our bikes and several other items we thought they could sell. Doña Angelica would be getting the other bike.

Sunday the 25th we took a ride with a taxi driver who'd driven us home from Actopan the last time we went to El Itacate, a great guy named Jesús. He spent about two hours with us, driving us up into the mountains behind Actopan for a close-up view of the rock formations called Los Frailes. I said I'd come back to the subject of Los Frailes (FRY-lehs), so here you go: Roughly, the legend of Los Frailes, and a nearby group of rock formations called Las Monjas (MOHN-hahs), is that one day, long ago, the friars of the convent of San Nicolás de Tolentino de Actopan went on a sojourn to visit the nuns from a convent in Mineral del Chico. The nuns, also, were going on a journey to visit the friars, and the plan was to meet somewhere in the middle. When they met, which was in the mountains above El Arenal, not far from Actopan, they got up to some hanky-panky there in the wilderness. To punish them, God turned them all to stone, and sentenced them, friars and nuns, to watch over and protect the Valle del Mezquital for all eternity. Harsh.

Getting back to our trip, after viewing Los Frailes, Jesús took us to a town called San Gerónimo, where there was a lake made by a dam, and hiked around it along with us, providing commentary on the history of the place. On the way back to Actopan, where we were planning to eat at El Itacate again, he stopped by his house and brought out several large crystals to give to Jon, since they'd established they were both rock collectors. I was worried about taking these heavy rocks back with us, but Jon said he'd make room.

From Jon: actually, I insisted.-)

The following Sunday, just four days before leaving, my sweet friend Daiset came to visit us with her partner Rina. Daiset is a lady I'd worked with via Zoom, basically just encouraging her to keep at the writing she'd already been doing. It was kind of like platonic love at first sight between us as we were so much on the same wavelength in terms of literature and writing.

Even though I was worried we wouldn't have time to hang out, since we were so busy packing up and all, Daiset insisted (clearly she has some of Jon's energy when it comes to determination). She drove up from Mexico City with Rina and their little dog to finally meet us in person. San Agustín was in the middle of a fair, so there was a lot going on in town besides the *tianguis*, and Daiset and Rina found it all totally charming. They bought tortillas from our favorite ladies to take home with them, declaring, just like Cecilia had, that San Agustín was the kind of town all Mexicans imagined the real Mexico was like.

I know that Daiset will be a life-long friend for me. She is also like Cecilia in that way though more academically-minded. She has been so grateful for the writing support I've given her though, honestly, I didn't think it was that much. Yet, she tells me she hadn't been writing until I met with her that first time via zoom but that, since then, she's been inspired all over again to finish projects that were important to her. She inspires me too, and anytime I feel a lag in energy to write, I will think of Daiset to spur me on.

Tuesday, the 30th, I had no plans to be at the school since teaching was done for me, though I hadn't gotten a chance to say good-bye to all the teachers. When I got a text from Rico in the morning, asking me if I planned to come, I knew something was afoot. I got there, as he requested, with Jon in tow, at 10:00. Cristina was there waiting for me in the office to gift me a large book of Mexican folk tales, and I had the chance to thank her again for the amazing friend and support she's been to me. (Can you feel me tearing up as I write this?)

Then, Jon, Rico and I wandered over to Docencia 2 together on some pretext that Rico had dreamed up. He's actually not very good at keeping a secret. We arrived at the upstairs room where I'd given my English workshops, to find all the teachers there, along with catered enchiladas, coffee, fruit, and juice awaiting us. I tried to act surprised though, truly, I was very moved. We ate and talked and laughed, until finally the teachers had to get to class. Some bestowed me with gifts and Rico made a short speech thanking me for my service at the school. Then it was my turn for a speech, first in English, since they're all English teachers, then in Spanish to really say, from the heart, how grateful I was to all of them.

Jon went home after that, but Rico asked me to drop by the office before I left. There, we had one last conversation, about my experience at the school, and his experience of my being there, speaking with total honesty. He wanted to know what could be improved at the school and with the teachers, and I wanted to know what I could have done better.

In that moment, I realized how much I would miss Rico and our heart-to-hearts, which we would sometimes have at the end of the day when he was sick of working, but before it was time for us to leave. He and I covered topics from sex education to marijuana and everything in between. He has proven to be a true friend to both me and Jon, someone we will always hold dear.

On the 31st, the town was celebrating the anniversary of the marketplace, which shows how important the daily marketplaces are in these small towns, and so we met Arlo and a friend of his from Mexico City for our last *tacos dorados* in the food court. As we wandered around the fair chatting, the friend told me he was surprised I had no American accent at all when I spoke Spanish, and that I sounded just like a Mexican. This was the greatest compliment anyone could pay me. I had finally achieved the level of Spanish I had been hoping I would during our time here.

Thursday morning, with broken hearts, we left San Agustín. Rico had arranged for Alberto and Lina to take us to the airport, just as they had driven us from CDMX to San Agustín at the beginning of it all. He even came to the house to see us off, and of course, Miriam, Maya, and Claudio were there to say good-bye. Doña Angelica was doing one final cleaning, and Marco came by with his mom, Maria, to "check over the house," to be sure we were leaving it in good shape. Are you kidding me? Considering we completely renovated it for him? I was sorry to leave with bad feelings for him, but nothing can change the love I have for Maria, and she and I parted with great affection.

I'm not going to go into how bad Alberto's navigation was on the way to the airport, how we ran into traffic jam after traffic jam, and how we made it to the airport with just enough time to spare; nor the three-hour delay in Los Angeles, nor how tired we were, nor how worried about Lupita being in her carrier for so long, nor the fact that I sobbed on the plane as it left Mexico.

We got home about 3:00 a.m. and all I could think was how beautiful our house was, while Lupita leapt to her favorite spot on the couch and settled right in. That night we slept, after taking showers with lots of hot water and great pressure, in our incredibly comfortable bed, preparing to assimilate back into the culture of the U.S., knowing it was not going to be easy.

Mexico was behind us now, but not for long. We would be back. It's in our blood, in our very souls. San Agustín will always be our place, and we will find a way to have a presence there again one day.

Epilogue: Steps Beyond Steps

Jon and I did go back, for 10 days during December of 2023, joined, for a few of those days, by my brother, Joshua. I wrote a blog post about it as a kind of epilogue to the blog/journal I kept during my Fulbright trip—a source for my friends and family members in the U.S. to keep up with what we were doing. I then used my blog while writing this book to help me remember all those things. Basically, the book is like an expanded version of the blog, which contains pictures of many of the places and people we mention here.

If you don't feel like going to the blog to find out if our December trip left us just as in love with San Agustín as before, the long and short of it is: it did. But, if you do want to read it, remember that the first page of the blog is the last entry so you'll see the post about the December trip first. To read the whole thing from the beginning, go here https://mexicofulbrightjourney.blogspot.com/, scroll to the bottom of the page, then select the date you want. The first one is from April, 2022.

Epilogue to Steps Beyond Steps

We ended up buying land just on the outskirts of San Agustín and hired a female, Mexican architect/builder to design and build a simple, but totally sustainable house for us there.

Also by Georgina Young-Ellis

The Time Mistress
The Time Baroness
The Time Heiress
The Time Contessa

Standalone
Darcy's Awakening
But For the Shadows, Mexico is Color

Watch for more at www.georginayoungellis.com.

Also by Jonathan Ellis

But For the Shadows, Mexico is Color

About the Author

Georgina is a published author of twelve novels, including a five-book time travel series, and eight works of Austenesque fiction. In 2022, Meryton Press published her World War II adaptation of *Pride and Prejudice,* called *Kiss Me Good Night, Major Darcy.* Before becoming a writer, Georgina was an actor. She is a member of the Screen Actors Guild, and has worked in television, film, commercials, and on stage. She has written and directed stage plays, and continues to work with writing partners on developing screenplays. Georgina holds a bachelor's degree in Theater from New York University and a master's degree in Spanish Language and Literature from Portland State University. She recently completed a Fulbright scholarship, which had her living and teaching in Hidalgo, Mexico for nine months, and working with Mexican female writers on a project to support and develop their literary voices.

Read more at www.georginayoungellis.com.

www.ingramcontent.com/pod-product-compliance
Lightning Source LLC
Chambersburg PA
CBHW051648040426
42446CB00009B/1032